THE REAL READER'S QUARTERLY

Slightly Foxed

'My Grandfather and Mr Standfast'

NO.44   WINTER 2014

Editors Gail Pirkis and Hazel Wood
Marketing and publicity Stephanie Allen and Jennie Paterson
Subscriptions Alarys Gibson, Anna Kirk, Faith McAllister and Olivia Wilson

Cover illustration: Mary Sumner, 'Sheep in frost'

Mary Sumner is an artist and printmaker who lives and works in mid-Devon. Her work
is rooted in her love for the English countryside and the creatures that inhabit it.
Observations from her daily walks inspire her paintings, and plants, seascapes and gardens
are also recurring themes. Her work can be seen in galleries throughout the UK and on
her website: www.marysumner.com.

Design by Octavius Murray

Layout by Andrew Evans

Colophon and tailpiece by David Eccles

Published by Slightly Foxed Limited
53 Hoxton Square
London N1 6PB

tel 020 7033 0258
fax 0870 1991245
e-mail all@foxedquarterly.com
www.foxedquarterly.com

Slightly Foxed is published quarterly in early March, June, September and December

Printed edition: annual subscription rates (4 issues)
UK £40; Europe £48; Rest of the World £52
Printed edition & digital edition: annual subscription rates
(4 issues plus digital access to all back issues)
UK £50; Europe £58; Rest of the World £62

Single copies of this issue can be bought for £10 (UK), £12 (Europe) or £13 (Rest of the World)

All back issues are also available: for details please ring 020 7033 0258 or visit our website
www.foxedquarterly.com

ISBN 978-1-906562-73-1

Printed and bound by Smith Settle, Yeadon, West Yorkshire

Contents

Contents

Howard Phipps, 'The Avenue, Odstock, in winter',
wood engraving

Our bookshop can obtain any of the books mentioned in this issue.
Slightly Foxed on Gloucester Road
123 Gloucester Road, London SW7 4TE
enquiries@foxedbooks.com
tel 020 7370 3503

From the Editors

Another year almost gone. The lights are going on early now in Hoxton Square, and on misty evenings there's a sense of a ghostly earlier London hovering just out of reach, while only a few hundred yards away down Old Street huge shiny office blocks are rising to create a new 'Tech City'. It's making us feel a bit ruminative. Thanks to Jennie and all the young staff, we're keeping up with and making good use of all the new technology, but we do also cling to what might be called 'old-fashioned' values – giving a really prompt and personal service to readers, keeping up our production standards, not cutting corners on writing and editing, and treating our suppliers and contributors decently. Thanks to you we've survived the recession, but things are still very tough for small businesses like *Slightly Foxed*, and our values do come at a cost.

We know they're important to you too, so we'd be very grateful if you could help us this Christmas by putting the word around to possible new subscribers, maybe giving someone a gift subscription or one of our books – you'll find a catalogue enclosed. And if you're buying other books, do remember the independent bookshops. Figures published earlier this year showed that for the first time there are now fewer than 1,000 of them left in Britain, and once gone they will never come back. Most of them, including our own shop on Gloucester Road, are run by people who love reading books rather than simply selling them: they provide a unique personal service, and they pay their taxes.

But enough already. The Fox is still in good shape, and we're delighted to be reissuing a beautiful and very distinctive book as our winter Slightly Foxed Edition – Gerald Durrell's *My Family and Other Animals* (see p.14). It's one of those books that speak to the child in us all – an evocation of a boyish paradise that has delighted readers of all ages since it was first published in 1956. For five years before the war, the Durrell family – the four children, Gerald, Larry, Leslie and Margo, and their mother – lived on Corfu, and here we see the famous naturalist as a boy, glorying in the freedom and beauty of the island, exploring its animal kingdom and getting to know a cast of characters quite as eccentric as his own eccentric family – and that includes the animals. It's both magical and funny – a perfect family book for reading aloud.

And speaking of books that appeal to readers of all ages, just a reminder that we're now halfway through our project of reissuing Ronald Welch's wonderful Carey chronicles, a series of historical novels that follow the same family from the Crusades to the tank battles of the First World War. Welch was a schoolmaster who wrote with children in mind, but there's no doubt that these books, in our elegant and highly collectable Cubs edition, are ringing bells with some of our older readers too. They're well-plotted, colourful and fascinatingly detailed, and give a great overview of the characters and pivotal campaigns of British history. You'll find them in the catalogue.

Also in the catalogue is another of our popular literary crosswords – the sixth. Entries should reach us no later than 14 January and the first correct one to be drawn out of a hat will receive a free annual subscription.

Thank you again for your support, your letters, your interest and your enthusiasm, which have meant so much to us in our tenth anniversary year. We wish you all a very peaceful Christmas, however you are spending it, and the best of good reading in 2015.

GAIL PIRKIS & HAZEL WOOD

My Grandfather and Mr Standfast

URSULA BUCHAN

The way things are going, we shall spend the next four years in tears. The commemorations of the First World War centenary depict the trenches on the Western Front as appalling places where young, promising men died in unimaginable horror, possibly for no, or the wrong, purpose: all was sorrow, regret and pointlessness.

In the hope that there might be other, more nuanced narratives, I have set myself the goal of reading widely about the war: recent histories, of course, but also those books written during it or soon after its end, since they more truly encapsulate the thoughts of those who went through it all. This naturally means the war poetry as well as the prose works of Sassoon, Graves and Blunden, but also *Mr Standfast*, my grandfather John Buchan's third Richard Hannay story, and his four-volume *History of the Great War*.

In 1914, John Buchan was 39 and an established publisher, writer and Parliamentary candidate. That summer, plagued by duodenal ulcers, he went with his family to Broadstairs to convalesce by the sea. There he wrote *The Thirty-Nine Steps*, published in October 1915, when it was an immediate success. In the autumn of 1914 his application to join the Army was turned down, so he suggested to Thomas Nelson, the Edinburgh publishing company of which he was a partner, that it issue a history of the war in monthly parts. Hilaire Belloc agreed to write it but then dropped out, so Buchan was forced to undertake the work himself. The result was *Nelson's History of the War*, published in

John Buchan, *Mr Standfast* (1919), is included in *The Complete Richard Hannay Stories* · Wordsworth · Pb · 992pp · £1.99 · ISBN 9781840226553.

24 volumes, the first appearing in February 1915. The royalties he gave to the families of the firm's employees away at the war.

In early 1915, *The Times* employed him as a war correspondent, and he reported on the second Battle of Ypres. That autumn, he was sent by the Foreign Office to observe the Battle of Loos. The next year, he was seconded to General Haig's headquarters in France to draft communiqués and then in July, while still in France, commissioned into the Intelligence Corps, principally handling press matters.

In early 1917, he was recalled and made Director of a Department of Information answerable only to the War Cabinet. In late 1917, the Prime Minister, David Lloyd George, turned the Department into a Ministry of Information under Lord Beaverbrook, with Buchan as Director of Intelligence. In the next two years, he visited Flanders and France a number of times. It was an intensely pressured and anxious job, particularly for a man who valued truth so highly, and it was not helped by the unpredictability and self-serving instincts of the politicians and newspaper barons with whom he had to deal.

But the very worst day of those years for him was 9 April 1917, when both his younger brother Alastair and his friend and business partner, Tommy Nelson, were killed at the Battle of Arras, within half a mile of each other. Buchan may not have been a combatant, but he had seen the fighting at first hand, and he had more than his share of sorrow, with a number of his greatest friends dying in the conflict.

At the end of the war, he was given the task of winding up the Department, and did it so carefully that scarcely a trace of its work remained (much to the frustration of later historians). In his autobiography, *Memory Hold-the-Door*, he describes his war mainly in terms of the loss of friends, as well as the battle he had to fight with his digestive system. In the process, he thoroughly downplays his own considerable contribution – partly, I suspect, out of modesty and partly because most of what he had done was highly secret.

Something we do know is that he wrote his 'shockers' for recreation, and it's not implausible to conclude that they also helped console him for not having fought in the trenches. There is certainly much emphasis in the wartime novels on courage, endurance and self-sacrifice, virtues he exhibited all his life, even if he never went 'over the top'.

He also used his wartime novels to say things that could not find a place in the patriotic and purposely morale-boosting Nelson's *History* or even *The Times* – in particular about the futility of war, the bellicosity of some British Generals, the waste and confusion of battle, and the goodness of many Germans. There are sympathetic descriptions of a conscientious objector and a sufferer from severe shell-shock in *Mr Standfast*, and of the Kaiser in *Greenmantle*. Buchan may have valued patriotism and love of country very highly, and considered the fight a necessary one, but he was no blinkered jingoist.

Mr Standfast was written between July 1917 and July 1918 and published in 1919. In it, Richard Hannay, the Scottish/South African engineer and foiler of German plots in *The Thirty-Nine Steps* and *Greenmantle*, is called out of the trenches, where he has recently been promoted to Brigadier-General, and told by Sir Walter Bullivant (the War Office spymaster) that he's needed for something very secret and dangerous: he must pose as a South African pacifist, and await further orders. He eventually discovers that he has to get on the trail of a spy – a spy who turns out to have been one of the Black Stone gang from *The Thirty-Nine Steps*, whom everyone had thought dead and buried. This spy has organized a network of agents which is getting important information out of Britain to Germany.

John S. Blenkiron and Peter Pienaar from *Greenmantle* reappear in this book, but not Sandy Arbuthnot, although there is a female addition to the team of counter-spies in the shape of the lovely and intelligent Mary Lamington. They keep in contact with one another by using Bunyan's *Pilgrim's Progress* as a device for relaying coded information.

In some pretty unlikely but brilliantly captured cameos, Hannay falls in love in Gloucestershire, kicks his heels among pacifists in Letchworth, consorts with radical trades unionists in Glasgow, climbs perilously in the mountains of Skye, is chased by Scottish and English police, burgles a French château, tends to Peter Pienaar, now a wounded ex-airman, in Switzerland, and climbs a glaciated mountain col in a tearing hurry, before ending back in the trenches on the Western Front.

Fiction writers inevitably draw from their own experience, even if it's transmuted into something very different in their stories. Buchan, whose skill in describing landscape and weather was second to none, writes vividly about both the Cuillins of Skye and the Col des Hirondelles in the Alps, places he knew well from his mountaineering trips as a young man. His hero, Hannay, uses his military skills to disrupt a trench battle scene being shot on a film set in Yorkshire, which Buchan would have known at first hand from his war work. Moreover, he must have come across Clydeside radicals like Andrew Amos, when he lived in the Gorbals (his father was a Free Church of Scotland minister in what was probably the worst slum parish in Britain), as well as Boer hunters, such as Peter Pienaar, when he worked for Lord Milner in South Africa. And he gives his stomach troubles, and his love of playing Patience, to the appealing American engineer and agent John S. Blenkiron.

In the thrilling climax of the book, he cleverly integrates fictional events into a factual context with an extraordinarily vivid and exciting description of the great German offensive in March 1918, when Ludendorff's divisions made a major push east of Amiens, under cover of fog, and very nearly succeeded in breaking through. Amazingly, Buchan began *Mr Standfast* before these events took place. I wonder how many other possible endings his fertile brain had imagined.

The fascination of these interweavings of fact and fiction, as well as the blistering narrative pace and the deep seriousness of purpose, far outweigh for me the inevitable flaws of a book written at odd moments, when there was so much else going on: for example, the careless racial stereotyping which, though commonplace then, makes us wince now, as well as the love scenes which embarrass and mildly disturb. The piled-on coincidences don't trouble me but I do have a problem with the idea of a 'baddie' who can so completely change his features as to be unrecognizable. All that said, I can still never put the book down, once started, thanks to its narrative drive, surprisingly complex characterizations and dry wit.

These days, when we think of the Somme, it is 1 July 1916, the worst day for casualties in the history of the British Army, which comes immediately to mind. But the fighting south and north of the River Somme from 21 March to early April 1918 was desperate, and absolutely crucial to the outcome of the war. The French had their forces massed in Champagne, some distance to the south-east, thinking that that was where the push would come. But instead the Germans pressed west over old battlegrounds, intending to take Amiens and then have a free route to Abbeville and the sea, so out-flanking the Allied forces and capturing the railway lines to Paris. The British forces were woefully inadequate, with only half the divisions that the Germans had, and in places they were outnumbered by as much as four to one, stretched wafer-thin along a 40-mile front. The situation was extremely perilous. It was vital that the Germans never got to know how few were the defenders and their reserves, and that their opponents somehow retreated in good order, when they had to, but also stood firm in front of Amiens and Arras until the French arrived to reinforce them.

Hannay and his band have discovered from the captured master-mind of the spy network, the Graf von Schwabing, that the push will indeed be in Picardy. Hannay dashes back to the Front, is promoted to Major-General and takes command of a division south of Peronne, where the Somme turns west, a place about 30 miles due east of Amiens, where Mary Lamington is nursing in a hospital. He puts von Schwabing in the British trenches, so that he will discover what the war that he has promoted so assiduously is really like. Hannay's ragbag division, desperately short of trained reinforcements, encompasses – in homage to his dead brother Alastair, no doubt – a battalion of Royal Scots Fusiliers, and looks to me to be modelled on the 30th Division, commanded in 1918 by Major-General W. de l'A. Williams. I have not been able to discover whether Buchan ever knew him, although I expect he did, or whether he asked permission to fictionalize what was an extremely brave rearguard action.

Somehow, in the book – as in real life – the division manages to beat an orderly retreat, although the losses are severe. Among them is the brave pacifist Launcelot Wake, who finds peace for his unquiet soul in acting as a runner for Hannay, and who saves the day by swimming the Somme and warning the neighbouring division that the Germans are threatening to outflank Hannay's men. John S. Blenkiron and his American engineers do a sterling job digging trenches and even get involved in the fighting.

And finally, Peter Pienaar, the wounded RFC ace, takes to the air again . . . but I won't spoil it for you. All I will say is that he thereby proves himself to be not Mr Standfast, as he thinks he is, but Mr Valiant-for-truth, the finest character from the author's beloved *Pilgrim's Progress*. In real life, the Germans pushed the Allies back 40 miles but, exhausted and with overextended supply lines, they never got as far as Amiens. That August (a month after Buchan finished *Mr Standfast*) the Allies, with the help of the recently arrived Americans, counterattacked, and by November, Germany was suing for peace.

If you read the account of this battle in the novel, you can follow it on a Michelin road map. Only a few names have been changed. Even in the comparatively dry, considered and very detailed *History*, Buchan cannot help but make the account stirring. Of the desperate fighting on 23 March, for example, he wrote, 'Giddy with lack of sleep, grey with fatigue, tortured by the ceaseless bombardments, summoned at almost every hour to repel attacks on flank and rear, the British troops had shown a fortitude beyond all human praise.'

My grandmother recalled her husband's demeanour during this time, when the British were finally facing up to the real possibility of defeat by Germany:

> During the dark days of the German breakthrough in 1918, when Haig's dispatch containing the words 'Our backs are against the wall' had sent a shudder through the nation, Henry [Sir Henry Newbolt] described to me the lunch hour at the Athenaeum Club . . . When John came in, all heads turned in his direction and whispers were rife. 'How does he look today? Does he look more cheerful than yesterday?' Henry always said that John's imperturbable calm did not vary, and that this did a great deal to steady people.

I sometimes try to imagine the scene. My grandfather – short in stature, dapper in the uniform of a colonel in the Intelligence Corps, fine-boned, with an aquiline nose and a forehead lined by a prominent scar that dated from a childhood accident – enters the high-ceilinged dining-room, and the clatter of cutlery falls silent as he greets his friend Newbolt. The swells of the Athenaeum – no doubt, many of them men of public affairs – know that he's the man who has read all the Intelligence reports from France. No wonder they search his face for signs of anxiety, even despair. Surely, surely, at this time he has no leisure to mull over the ending of *Mr Standfast*? Or does he? The thought of it fair takes my breath away. It is, frankly, this collision of real and fictional drama that makes *Mr Standfast* more than just an enjoyable and interesting period piece. And it reminds me how profoundly I regret that I never had the chance to know my grandfather.

URSULA BUCHAN can, sadly, discern few common characteristics with her grandfather – except a weakness for tobacco (sternly suppressed), a troublesome digestion and a deep love of upland places.

Paradise Regained

SIMON BARNES

Every paradise is lost. That's kind of the point. Loss is the diagnostic feature of every paradise ever lived or imagined. But for five miraculous years and 120,000 miraculous words Gerald Durrell sustained a vision of paradise with joy in every day and every page. Most evocations of paradise dwell on the eventual loss: not here. *My Family and Other Animals* is a tale of uninterrupted delight. It finishes with a brief, almost apologetic admission that all such things come to an end – but in truth the book doesn't really end at all. It is just politely euthanized, a beloved family pet tactfully and efficiently put down by a trusted vet.

It's an account of five years that Durrell and his family spent on the Greek island of Corfu, departing in 1939 just ahead of the war. They left England on this mad jaunt 'like a flock of migrating swallows' and had what really was the time of their lives. It was the making of Gerald – Gerry in the book, the youngest of four, mad for wildlife and agog for all other kinds of life as well – and the book makes that abundantly clear. 'It was intended to be a mildly nostalgic account of the natural history of the island, but I made a grave mistake by introducing my family in the first few pages.' The family, riotous, bohemian, noisy, excessive, included Larry, or Lawrence Durrell, who later wrote *The Alexandria Quartet* – though I believe *My Family* is a more important and ultimately a more serious work.

I first read it as a boy and I lived it and loved it like a boy. I was Gerry among the rock-pools, Gerry climbing the swaying branches, Gerry lost in the wonders of nature, Gerry forever out of step with his own family – isolated by age and his unshared passion for the wild world – but Gerry enviably certain of perpetual love and support. I was also, though I didn't realize this at the time, Gerry discovering what life is all about and what really matters. That is to say, wildlife and family. The book adroitly balances these two things as if there were immense tensions between them, shifting from one subject to the other effortlessly, and with such skill that with each shift you are both satisfied and left wanting more. But at base the two subjects are united – in the title, in Gerry's love, and above all in that both are indispensable ingredients of paradise: "'*Chairete*," he called in his deep voice, the beautiful Greek greeting, "*Chairete, kyrioi* . . . be happy" . . . How could one be anything else in such a season?'

These two great subjects of wildlife and family life are brought together against the backdrop of the island of Corfu and the people who live there. Descriptions of landscape are notoriously skippable things, especially in a fattish book, but not here. I remember the mixture of awe and fellow-feeling when Durrell sees Corfu for the first time and the sea 'turned the smooth enamelled blue of a jay's eye'. I realized at once that this wasn't a book at all, in the normal sense of the term: it was a letter addressed to me personally, written with a deep, intimate knowledge of the sort of person I was and the sort of things I liked. I don't think this is a unique experience, either. It's that kind of book.

It reads like a tale of innocence, innocence of a rather knowing kind. Gerry is discovering the great wild world, but not without a little background knowledge. He is also discovering the great grown-up world and is allowed to share it far more than is usual for a child. He is extraordinarily privileged, then: privileged to have the wild world quite literally on his doorstep, and privileged to live in a family that allows him so many liberties. He is a child among grown-ups but never left out and never lonely; he is a child free to go where he pleases in the wild world and is always at home there. His readers are invited to share this double privilege and that is what makes the book so peculiarly intoxicating.

It reads like a great outpouring of love, flowing like a pell-mell mountain stream, unstoppable, ungovernable, random, untamed and utterly spontaneous. It doesn't read as if it had been written by a writer at all: it's as if it had sprung fully formed from the mind of a rather knowing child, as if Durrell the author had taken dictation from the young Gerry. And while something of that is the case, it is by no means the whole story.

Daniel Macklin

My Family and Other Animals, published in 1956, is the work of a very fine writer at the very peak of his powers. This was Durrell's sixth book; he was an established bestselling author who really knew his craft. It is constructed with immense and conscious skill, with a complex double chronology few writers could bring off. The passage from one villa to the next punctuates the five-year time-span of the family's stay on Corfu, while the movement of the seasons of a single year gives the loose aggregation of incidents a natural rhythm that unites the book from front to back.

It was never intended as a literal account of the Durrell family's time on the island. The material is arranged for literary convenience in the way that an architectural painter will make judicious omissions and alterations to what he sees in front of him. This is not cheating, for literalness can obscure meaning. Rather, this is a careful rearrangement that reveals a greater truth than mere facts. For example, brother Larry's wife Nancy is written out of the book. She and Larry mostly had their own establishment on Corfu, but for literary purposes Larry is single again and back with the family. The book is full of additions, subtractions, reimaginings, exaggerations; in the two later Corfu books, *Birds, Beasts and Relatives* and *The Garden of the Gods* – pleasant reading, very pleasant, but not the masterpiece we have here – these become quite shameless.

Durrell had been talking, and more importantly thinking, about the book for years before he wrote it. He finally sat down to do so in the knowledge that this was the best material he would ever have and he would never be in better shape to write it. He did so mostly in a frenzied six-week period in Bournemouth in a room in the boarding-house run by his sister Margaret, Margo in the book. The book was meticulously planned, and each character had his character-notes. ('Larry: unctuous, posey, humorous. Mother: vague, harassed.') There was nothing flukey about *My Family*. Its spontaneity is the result of conscious craft. It was written by an accomplished author writing in the sure and certain knowledge that in more than one sense he was writing the book of his life.

Durrell often found writing a bit of a chore: a necessary task that helped with what he saw as far more important work: making wildlife collecting expeditions and, subsequently, running the Jersey Wildlife Preservation Trust (now the Durrell Wildlife Conservation Trust) which uses the zoo he established on Jersey as a base for all kinds of practical conservation. *My Family* was the great exception: it was a book he wrote with joy. You don't need to read Douglas Botting's excellent biography (called simply *Gerald Durrell: The Authorised Biography*) to know that.

My Family and Other Animals is about learning, and so it is also about teachers. There are the false teachers, the tutors who seek to force formal education on a boy who would far sooner be out in the olive groves looking for caterpillars. But there are also the real teachers. The most obvious is Theo, Corfiot, doctor and naturalist, who shows Gerry how to organize his wild enthusiasm into a coherent understanding of the wild world. Gerry's mother is herself an education in tolerance, indulgence and love. The third great tutor exists only in hints: Larry, the great writer (in real life his brother's constant encourager), shows him that writing is something that matters, and something that can be attacked by those with the will to do so.

When you read the book in maturity – and it is a book to be read again and again, and then read to your children – you naturally find new things. Behind the riotous family parties, the glorious swathes of wild landscape and the wild creatures who live in it and invade the family home, you find a book about fragility. Two different sorts of fragility, in fact. The first is childhood: all childhoods, however glorious, must end: childhood happiness is by definition doomed. The second is the fragility of the wild world. Neither of these is much touched on – it's as if both could go on forever – but both are there at the book's heart. The fragility of the wild world is something we all live with these days. This was something Durrell understood long before most people, and he dedicated his life to the protection of that world: 'People think I'm trying to look after fluffy animals,' he once said. 'I'm actually trying to stop the human race from committing suicide.' This great issue was to bring Durrell to despair and break-down, later to recovery and renewal in his second marriage.

Durrell was a great writer, but he would hate to be remembered as such. He was also a great conservationist, and his sense of mission drove everything he did. In his view, his writing was good insofar as it helped conservation: by spreading his ideas and by telling the world about the Durrell Wildlife Conservation Trust. He often wrote in strong and campaigning terms about the state of the world and he did as much to spread the notion that wildlife conservation matters as any one who ever drew breath.

But one of his greatest contributions to the conservation movement is *My Family and Other Animals*. It is not about conservation save by implication: what it does is to tell us – vividly and unforgettably and joyously – that the world and the people who live in it are infinitely richer for the wild places and the wild creatures we share it with. The wild world completes us, makes us whole, and brings us joy. The wild world is – or should be – what truly completes the family circle.

SIMON BARNES writes on wildlife and sport. He spent more than 30 years with *The Times* and has written 20-odd books, including the bestselling *Bad Birdwatcher* trilogy. His latest, *Ten Million Aliens*, is about the entire animal kingdom. He lives in East Anglia with his family and other animals.

Gerald Durrell's *My Family and Other Animals* (384pp) is now available from *Slightly Foxed* in a new limited and numbered cloth-bound pocket edition of 2,000 copies, each priced at £16 (UK), £18 (Europe) or £19 (Rest of the World). All prices include post and packing. Copies may be ordered by post (53 Hoxton Square, London N1 6PB), by phone (020 7033 0258) or via our website www.foxedquarterly.com.

Aunt Freda Opens a Door

ANTHONY WELLS

One day in the late 1980s I had a call from my Aunt Freda. It came completely out of the blue, for although Freda had been my favourite godmother throughout my childhood, I had hardly exchanged a word with her – save the odd Christmas card – for what must have been twenty years. The purpose of her call was to tell me she had a box of books to give me and would I like to pick them up from my parents' house in Sheffield, where she would drop them off on her next visit. 'There's a complete Shakespeare, Churchill's *Island Race* and an encyclopaedia,' she said by way of brief explanation.

Books were not the first thing I associated with Freda, a thorough-going countrywoman, a horse-rider and dog-breeder, who farmed a few acres in the wilds of North Yorkshire. Her reading matter was more likely to be *Horse & Hound* and *Bantam Breeder's Weekly* than *The Good Companions* or even *Wuthering Heights*. Nevertheless, she had been a godparent nonpareil for a compelling reason: her Christmas presents were in a league of their own. So spurred partly by duty and partly by her track record as a present-giver, I gladly accepted the books and drove up to Sheffield to collect them. As soon as I looked in the box, I realized that Freda had lost none of her class in the gift department. *The Island Race* was a large-format edition with lavish illustrations; the Shakespeare was a facsimile First Folio; and the encyclopaedia was the 24-volume, half-leatherbound, gilt top-edged 14th (1929) edition of *The Encyclopaedia Britannica*.

The Encyclopaedia Britannica! While Shakespeare and *The Island Race* had been on the bookshelves in one form or another when I was young, this would be the first time I had shared living-space with a

Britannica. From childhood I remembered the *Pears Cyclopaedia* –
cyclopaedia, incidentally, being 'an etymologically meaningless word,
stigmatized as an inferior form by G. J. Vossius in "De vitiis sermonis
1645"', according to the *Oxford Dictionary of English Etymology* – and,
dimly, Arthur Mee's *Children's Encyclopaedia*. From schooldays, I
recalled the *Oxford Illustrated Dictionary* and from university only the
tip that, if you had spent the previous eight terms a complete stranger
to lecture halls and libraries, boning up on the relevant entries in *The
Encyclopaedia Britannica* could scrape you a second. (When, later, on
an MA course I had to compare two editions of the *Britannica* for an
essay, I understood why there might be something in this tip: the
chances were the entry had been written by your professor.)

Thus it was that for the first time I became the proud possessor of
the 'greatest encyclopaedia in the English language'. J. L. Garvin, the
editor of the – my – 14th edition, ushered me into the *Britannica*
world in his preface:

> This Edition, then, is the Fourteenth of the series which began
> with the modest issue of six-penny numbers ('or 8d on fine
> paper,' said the Edinburgh printers) in December 1768 when
> George III was King. The talk was all of Mr Wilkes and of
> floods higher than could be remembered, spreading in many
> counties 'like a sea'.

Floods spreading like a sea? So what's new, the early twenty-first
century reader is likely to ask, recalling the television pictures from
the Somerset Levels. And 'what's new', as it happens, is the essential
question confronting any encyclopaedia editor as he contemplates
the prospect of a new edition. Here are Mr Garvin's reflections in
1929:

> The map of the intellectual world, more than that of the polit-
> ical, is changed beyond recognition. On every side we see new
> mechanisms and agencies with consequent new social activities

and habits: in many ways we are farther from the youth of our grandparents, even from the youth of our parents, than were they from the middle ages . . .

The expansion of knowledge in the mere twenty years that had passed since the previous landmark edition – the 11th of 1911 – required 'a bold departure from precedent and a fundamental change in the method of encyclopaedia-making', according to Garvin. It was no longer possible, as it still just about had been in 1911, for any one man or even one central staff to map out the world of contemporary knowledge, with its 'major and minor configurations and boundaries'. Knowledge was now too vast and too subdivided, too many new fields and sub-fields had sprung up; in science alone 'the difference between the Eleventh Edition and its present successor is like an advance not of twenty years but of a hundred'.

Garvin's solution to encompassing this explosion of knowledge in so many fields was to delegate the task to teams of specialist editors, each a monarch in his own realm. Formally, his solution was to divide each corpus of knowledge into a more differentiated range of headings, some as in the great 11th edition almost of book length but many more of only a few paragraphs. This would make the *Britannica* a much handier work of ready reference than before. To complement these changes, the new edition added a larger and more refined index and would be furnished 'with every resource of illustration', as Garvin boasted.

Marshalled by the two staffs of editors, one in London, the other in New York – the 14th was the second joint Anglo-American *Britannica* – was a team of 3,000 contributors 'from across the world'. A glance down the names singled out by Garvin for special mention conveys their calibre. Under the arts, Roger Fry on Cézanne, Max Reinhardt and Constantin Stanislavski on Theatre, Donald Tovey on Beethoven; under the sciences, J. B. S. Haldane on heredity, Niels Bohr on the atom, Ernest Rutherford on radioactivity and one Dr Einstein on space-time; Bernard Shaw and G. D. H. Cole on socialism, Baden-Powell on boy scouts; philosophers Benedetto Croce on aesthetics, Ernst Cassirer on transcendentalism and Edmund Husserl on phenomenology (where, the editor notes, the author writes 'as an originator'); Gilbert Murray on Greek drama, J. B. Priestley on the English Romantics, G. K. Chesterton on humour and Lion Feuchtwanger on the modern novel; under history, Ernest Barker on the Crusades, John Addington Symonds on the Renaissance and on US financial history no less an authority than the Hon. Andrew W. Mellon, 'secretary of the Treasury under three administrations'. The roll-call makes clear just how eager were the editors to enlist the top names in each field, not only academics but also men and women of action, and likewise how much pride these men and women attached to being asked to contribute.

Their erudition and experience aside, these people could write. The readability for which the 11th edition of the *Britannica* has so often been praised was retained by its successor. One might suppose that the purpose of an encyclopaedia is simply to provide information, that content is king and the form neither here nor there. But the best *Britannicas* give the lie to this. The 11th and 14th editions both contain articles of such authority and style that they readily stand the test of time; indeed some are so informative, balanced and well-written they have been separately anthologized and reprinted.

Its readability is one of the reasons why my Aunt Freda's gift of the 1929 *Britannica* – its 24 volumes, each 1,000 pages long, containing a total of 35,000,000 words – still occupies an honoured place on my bookshelves. But, you might ask, isn't it now completely out of date? Surely the 14th edition of 1929 was made redundant by its successor the 15th in 1974, just as the 14th had replaced the 11th?

Sort of, but not really. First, as Garvin wrote in his preface, every such undertaking as a general encyclopaedia is 'a sort of landmark in the history of knowledge' and of interest as such. Second, certain kinds of knowledge barely increase from one generation to another, or only in minor or inconsiderable ways: the early history of Alexandria is still much as it was in 1929 and the geological features of my native Sheffield and its environs haven't changed hugely in the interim either. Even for rapid reference, this seemingly antiquated work comes in handy: a short way into Edmund de Waal's *The Hare with Amber Eyes* I ran to the Index for 'netsuke' and was directed to Ivory Carving (Vol. 12) and the charming examples in Plate VIII.

More seriously, my 1929 *Britannica* offers an even more profound example of how exaggerated our opinion of our intellectual or scholarly progress may prove to be. The other great change that fell between 1911, the year of the previous edition, and 1929, besides those in science and the 'mechanisms and customs of life', as Garvin calls them, was the World War. 'The interval', he wrote, 'is like an abyss between two political epochs. A rending convulsion continues its influence upon the circumstances and the thought of mankind.'

Garvin – who, like Kipling, lost his only son in the conflict – gave ample space in his new edition to a consideration of the war, of its causes, conduct, conclusion and legacy. The task of co-ordinating and ordering the contributions, extending to 'some hundreds of articles and some thousands of pages', was handed to Captain B. H. (Basil) Liddell Hart, as associate editor, with different aspects considered by, among others, Marshal Foch, General Pershing, Colonel Fuller and Colonel T. E. Lawrence. What is striking when one reads these *Britannica* articles now, 85 years later, on the centenary of the war's outbreak, is how little the overall assessment has changed. The summary of C. Seignobos, professor of history at the Sorbonne, of the 'question of responsibility' might have been written last week:

It is certain that no government really desired a European war . . . The governments of the three empires wished to avert a general war but they were too distrustful of one another frankly to consult upon the means of avoiding it; for each feared to reveal its plan lest it should become the dupe of a bluff or ruse.

France and England were powerless spectators of the conflict. France was bound by the Russian alliance; the British cabinet did not dare to risk action which had not been approved by the nation. The war was not the work of personal ambitions but the result of the system of the three military empires, Austria, Russia and Germany . . .

The point is not whether this is the 'right' view but that a view so familiar to us today was already fully formed and being persuasively set out in time to be published as part of the 24-volume *Britannica* in 1929.

A further warning against the assumption that, because we come after, we necessarily know better, is offered by the subsequent history of the *Britannica* itself. In 1974 a new team of editors took it upon themselves to reinvent the entire work. In an act of supreme hubris, made worse by their condescension towards their distinguished predecessors and their dismissal of the great 11th Edition as 'little more than a historical novelty of interest largely to sentimentalists', these brave new editors came up with a newfangled arrangement which turned out to be messier, more obscure and less manageable than either of its immediate predecessors, as well as being less readable and more poorly printed. It is only just that their (15th) edition has now itself passed into history, superseded not by a later printed edition but by an entire new technology: for the *Britannica*, like the *OED*, now has only a virtual existence.

What Hazlitt said about new books – that he preferred to read old ones – turns out to apply almost as well to encyclopaedias, or to the *Britannica* at least. Can my late Aunt Freda possibly have read Hazlitt?

After a 25-year career divided between the BBC World Service and London's Wiener Library, ANTHONY WELLS now devotes as much time to writing as running a small family business allows.

Educating Ulyth

YSENDA MAXTONE GRAHAM

On the cobwebby bathroom bookshelf of our family's shabby but adored flat in Avignon sits a book which I have read 44 times – once a year since first going to the flat in 1970. Wedged in between *The Damon Runyon Omnibus* and *Don't Tell Alfred*, it's a thick-papered hardback girls' school story called *For the Sake of the School*, by Angela Brazil, and for me it never palls.

It really should have palled by now, as Brazil has some fairly terrible stylistic habits. For example, she avoids the word 'said' in her dialogue-filled prose, substituting for it multiple elegant variations such as 'propounded Marjorie Butler', 'piped Romola Harvey', 'volunteered Consie' and 'ejaculated Lindsay'. Her depictions of the heavily scented English countryside, in which most of her fictional girls' boarding-schools are set, are chocolate-box-lid florid. Her thumbnail sketches of her characters and their schoolmistresses are fairly repetitive: there's many a 'flaxen-haired damsel' who, 'if not exactly pretty, knew how to make the best of herself'; and many a strict spinster headmistress with 'iron-grey hair'. The names she gives her girls are a formulaic juxtaposition of the romantic and the plain: Ernestine Salt, Blanche Greenwood, Raymonde Armitage, Morvyth Holmes, Fauvette Robinson. The heroine of *For the Sake of the School* is Ulyth Stanton, and she addresses her mother as 'Motherkins' in her letters home.

Angela Brazil, *The Manor House School* (1910), *The School by the Sea* (1914), *For the Sake of the School* (1915), *The Luckiest Girl in the School* (1916), *For the School Colours* (1918) and *A Patriotic Schoolgirl* (1918) are out of print but are available as e-books on Project Gutenberg.

I think what hooks me, and many of us who adore girls' school stories, is the deep longing to belong and be accepted by a gaggle of girls. And not just any girls: girls who (like us) get a thrill out of embroidered nightdress cases, matching writing-paper and envelopes, autograph books, china ornaments, photograph frames, and brush and comb sets. The thought of stepping out of the train at Llangarmon Junction in September 1915, into a crowd of such schoolgirls looking for each other – 'There's Helen!' 'And Ruth, surely!' 'Oh! Where's Marjorie?' – is delicious to anyone who finds the word 'dormitory' or even 'cubicle' exciting. We are stepping into a clearly defined world, where the rules are set in stone and where the headmistress, when we get into trouble, will be 'not angry, just deeply grieved'.

I hardly need tell you that 'Brazil' is supposed to be pronounced 'Brazzle', although I still find it hard not to pronounce it as it looks. Unmarried, childless, but busy and fulfilled, Angela Brazil (1869–1947) lived in Coventry (a place to which some of her characters are metaphorically and unwillingly sent), and most of her romantic inclinations, it seems, were channelled into celebrating the romance of life in a girls' boarding-school, which she distilled into 59 novels. Unlike Elinor Brent-Dyer's Chalet School and Enid Blyton's Malory Towers books, Brazil created a totally fresh school for each novel: The Dower House, The Manor House, The Woodlands, Aireholme, Brackenfield, Silverside, Birkwood Grange and so on.

'The summer term was always of more than usual interest.' So starts a paragraph in *The School by the Sea*, describing life at The Dower House. 'The school lived mostly out of doors, many classes were held in the garden, and meals, when weather permitted, were often taken on the lawn.' Don't you long to be there, in your linen afternoon dress, listening to 'the soft thud of tennis balls and distant cries of "Vantage!" and "Game!"'? I certainly do. 'What a frolicsome notion!' as one of the schoolgirls would say.

Brazil's first novel, *A Terrible Tomboy*, was published in 1904 and she wrote two books a year till the last one, *The School on the Loch*, in 1946. I've been looking at the ones she wrote during the First World War, from *The School by the Sea* (1914) to *A Patriotic Schoolgirl* (1918). As well as being highly readable stories, they show how that war gradually impinged on the daily lives of the fictional schoolgirls of Britain, who in 1915 were merely knitting socks and doing a bit of bandaging practice, but by 1918 were visiting munitions factories, hunting down German spies, dispensing with servants, eating 'war cake conspicuous by its lack of sugar', planting vegetable plots and making scrap albums for the hospital.

I have yet to find any of Brazil's novels quite as satisfying, purely from the point of view of the plot, as *For the Sake of the School* (1915), which is illuminating for anyone interested in the unformed characters of girls. Ulyth Stanton, exquisitely well brought up, deeply proud of her school The Woodlands, longing to be a member of its Camp Fire League, waits excitedly for the arrival of her penfriend from New Zealand, Rona Mitchell, with whom she's going to be sharing her cubicle. When Rona arrives at the school after her sea voyage across the globe, 'there was a noise such as nobody had ever heard at The Woodlands before'. That noise is the sound of Rona's hideously loud (and nasal) colonial voice, and her 'hinnying laugh'. The story tells how Ulyth deals with her shock and disappointment; how the headmistress (Miss Bowes) doesn't let Ulyth swap rooms; how the even more snooty Stephanie Radford is first vile to Rona and then knocked down a peg or two; how the friendship between Ulyth and Rona gradually develops; and how Rona, the rough diamond, is polished and eventually discovered to be of very noble birth.

As well as being carried along by the plot, I devour every paragraph of Brazil's novels for details of what girls' boarding-schools were like then. For one thing, although they were housed in manor-houses and castles, their numbers were tiny: 30 girls at the Manor House School; 39 at Silverside in *For the School Colours* (that is, before the invasion of the local day-girls, which annoys the boarders

Daniel Macklin

and makes a good story); and only 26 at Marlowe Grange (*The Madcap of the School*). Brazil never tires of describing school traditions and rules, and no detail is too small to include – such as the names of dormitories (the Cowslip Room) or the precise stitches used in sewing (open-hem stitch). The girls change for dinner every evening. They don't go home at all during term-time. Their letters home are censored. In the summer term they go blackberrying: in *For the Sake of the School* there is a chapter called 'A Blackberry Foray', in which Rona gets stuck in a tree-trunk and says a great deal in her loud nasal voice. ('Well, I guess that's taken the bounce out of me. I'm as stiff as a rheumatic cat! Oh, I'll get back to school somehow, don't alarm yourself.')

If you have read Victorian boys' school stories, such as Dean Farrar's *Eric, or Little by Little*, where many of the boys' scrapes and japes end either with a caning or an actual death, it is a relief, with Angela Brazil, to be in a world where the sound of the headmistress's footsteps coming closer in the middle of the night heralds nothing worse than a mortifying torrent of moralistic words. 'This afternoon's occurrence has grieved me more than I can express,' or, 'Have you been here a whole term, Avelyn, and not yet learnt the very elements of honour?' The female reader strongly feels the 'Ouch!' of such words, and even blushes along with Avelyn.

The harshest punishment in all the First World War novels is this one, from Mrs Morrison to Marjorie Anderson in *A Patriotic Schoolgirl.* Marjorie, out of genuine pity and a desire to be kind, has written to, and received a letter back from, Private Hargreaves, a lonely soldier in France of whom she has heard. Receiving letters from anyone except parents or guardians is strictly against the school rules. 'Every pupil', says Mrs Morrison to Marjorie, 'is at least supposed to be a gentlewoman, and that a Brackenfielder could so demean herself as to enter into a vulgar correspondence with an unknown soldier fills me with disgust and contempt. I cannot keep such a girl in the school. You will go for the present to the isolation room, and remain there until I can make arrangements to send you home.' Marjorie, thank goodness, is granted a reprieve, for which she is profoundly thankful. Little would Brazil have known how powerfully Mrs Morrison's disdainful words 'an unknown soldier' would resonate a century later.

Usually the punishments are merely tedious tasks such as copying out the whole of 'Lycidas' or Bacon's essay 'Of Empire', learning two pages of Curtis's *Historical Notes* by heart, or being sent to bed straight after supper instead of being allowed to go to the Needlework Union. 'If Bunty puts me to construe anywhere on page 21 I'm a gone coon,' complains a post-punishment Manor House schoolgirl, reminding us that we are also in shockingly pre-politically-correct days here. Some of the girls collect golliwogs. In *The Jolliest Term on Record* we read that 'Gwethyn liked drawing animals, or niggers, or copying funny pictures from comic books.'

We are also in pre-health-and-safety days. The girls carry naked candles up old oak staircases to bed. Their possessions catch fire, and lives are saved by quick reflexes. The girls rush, unattended by adults, down to the lake or sea to bathe, and many of them can't swim.

Again, lives are saved by the stronger, swimming girls. In *The Luckiest Girl in the School* there's a hair-raising episode in which the 16-year-old Winona Woodward is allowed to drive her Aunt Harriet's motor-car around the local country lanes, never having driven a car before. 'Winona never knew by how much she exceeded the speed-limit,' Brazil merrily writes.

For what are these girls being educated? Brazil is vague about this, but there's little (if any) mention of university, and one senses that a good marriage is the hoped-for outcome. The most academic school in Brazil's 1914–18 novels is the urban day-school in *The Luckiest Girl in the School*, Seaton High School, to get into which Winona Woodward has to sit two days of stiff exams – in fact she and another girl both drop their entry forms so they get mixed up and Winona is mistakenly given a place. (Brazil makes the spot-on observation that 'Mrs Woodward was one of those parents who expect their children to gain the prizes which they were incapable of winning for themselves.') Winona's reaction, on being entered for the school, is 'But I don't want to win scholarships and go in for a career!' She has to work extremely hard at Seaton High, studying Virgil all evening while also finding time to practise her Schubert Impromptus and Bach Preludes and Fugues.

At the girls' boarding-schools, by contrast, one feels that a bit of French-speaking with Mademoiselle, a spot of Latin and maths (or 'maths.' – it still has a full stop), a great deal of drawing and painting, a sound knowledge of the acceptable works of English literature, and the occasional dabbling in chemistry in the more forward-looking schools, will be quite adequate. Plus, of course, the endless tennis, hockey, cricket and calisthenics. But you feel that the girls are, actually, getting a wonderful education. The thing is, they love it. This surely must help. They adore romantic English literature and romantic English history. When it's discovered that Winona Woodward only got her place at Seaton High School because of a mix-up, the headmistress has another look at her entrance exam papers, and the single thing that saves her is that she wrote a marvellous, deeply imagined, romantic essay on what it must have been like to be Lady Jane Grey. This is typical of an Angela Brazil schoolgirl. The girls adore *The Lady of the Lake*, they are enraptured by any girl with 'long, glossy Burne-Jones hair', and they always plait garlands of flowers on May Day.

To write this, I brought *For the Sake of the School* back to London with me from Avignon, in order to read it for the 45th time. It looks totally out of place in England and must now be taken back to its rightful spot in a bathroom in Provence.

YSENDA MAXTONE GRAHAM had to learn the hymn 'Lead us, heavenly Father, lead us' by heart as a punishment at her girls' boarding prep school in the 1970s. She wonders whether hymn-learning is ever still used as a punishment.

The Importance of Being Decent

MATTHEW ADAMS

In January 1939, as Europe was convulsing to the rhythms of what George Orwell would call 'the tom-tom beat of a latter-day tribalism', W. H. Auden, Christopher Isherwood and E. M. Forster were gathered at Waterloo Station. It was a solemn occasion. Auden and Isherwood were about to leave the country of their birth for the United States, where, several months later, Auden would compose 'September 1, 1939', the ominous poem in which he would look back on 'the low dishonest decade' he had just lived through, and tremble at the one to come. Auden and Isherwood attracted much criticism for their decision to leave England at so crucial an hour, yet Forster refused to abandon his friends. As he bade them farewell at Waterloo, he told them that it was now their duty to 'keep away' and 'see us sink from a distance'. It would be his duty, he continued, 'to face a world which is tragic without becoming tragic myself'.

When Forster spoke those words he was in his sixties. He had published no fiction for over a decade, partly because of his 'weariness of the only subject that I both can and may treat – the love of men for women & vice versa'. What he had wanted to publish was the kind of work in which 'two men should fall in love and remain in it for the ever and ever that fiction allows', yet he did not feel able to risk the obloquy that would have followed. He did, however, continue to write on that theme in private. There were numerous short stories, there was the novel *Maurice*, published posthumously in 1971, and dedicated 'to a happier year'. And there were great swathes of

E. M. Forster, *Two Cheers for Democracy* (1951), is out of print.

criticism, essays and broadcasts. The first collection of these had been published in 1936 under the title *Abinger Harvest*; the second would not appear until 1951. Yet at the moment Forster stood in solidarity with his friends on that January day at Waterloo, he was already at work on the pieces of which the volume would be composed, already addressing himself to a world that looked increasingly tragic.

That volume would become *Two Cheers for Democracy*. Now long out of print (the most recent edition was published in 1970), it was initially to be called *The Last of Abinger*, yet Forster changed his mind on the grounds that he did not really want to record the last of any-thing, and because the new title – offered as a joke by a young friend – appealed to him. It seemed to strike an appropriate note of cautious optimism. 'Human life is still active, still carrying about with it unex-plored riches and unused methods of release,' he writes in the preface: 'The darkness that troubles us and tries to degrade us may thin out. We may still contrive to raise three cheers for democracy, although at present she only deserves two.'

So: 'Two Cheers for Democracy'. As I suspect is true of others, I had encountered the phrase (and felt slightly sniffy about it) long before I had read the book in which it appears. I had read and enjoyed Forster's novels in my teens, but – for reasons not altogether clear to me now – I hadn't read a word of his non-fiction. It wasn't that I expected something dry or solemn, and I knew that Kingsley Amis was not being fair when he dismissed him (quite amusingly) as a 'cheerless crap'. Forster's non-fiction was simply a blind spot, and would remain one, I am ashamed to say, all the way through my undergraduate degree in English. The moment of introduction came in the early days of my doctoral research. I was working on the radi-cal writing of the 1640s, and had been told that Forster had written a piece to mark the tercentenary of Milton's *Areopagitica* (1644), collected in *Two Cheers for Democracy*. With no very great sense of excitement, I called the book up at the Bodleian and dutifully trudged off to see what he had to say.

It would be overstating things to describe what followed as a revelation, but it was something like a gradual process of awakening. The piece on *Areopagitica* was interesting enough, but what captivated me was the range and tone of the other essays and broadcasts that made up the book. Here was a figure who offered much of what I felt was missing from my academic life – and much of what I loved of life in general. Where those around me seemed interested largely in becoming specialized and establishing themselves as grand figures in their field, Forster was roaming, understated, modest, unemphasized. He became my companion. From now on, my days roosting in the Bodleian would be leavened by a spell in the pub with *Two Cheers for Democracy*. And if I went for a drink in the evening, Forster would come along too. I carried him everywhere. And as I read and reread him on the many subjects covered in his book, I came to realize that I was encountering elements of a personality that were present in the personalities of those I knew, and loved, myself, and were perhaps not so pronounced in my own person as they might have been. Forster was calm, curious, sane, gentle, amused, ordinary. And I, gentle reader, was being edified.

One of the first things to strike me was Forster's sense of commitment – both to his subjects and to his readers, and to the relationship between politics and the arts. The pieces in the book, written over a period of fifteen years, are arranged thematically rather than chronologically, and are grouped into two broad sections. The first part of the book, 'The Second Darkness', concentrates on the political and social questions relating to the Second World War, including anti-Semitism, the nature of tolerance, censorship and liberty. The second, 'What I Believe', is more various, and features pieces on *not* looking at pictures, on writers and poets, on our second greatest novel, on his library, on place – and, of course, on belief.

So far, so various – yet almost all the pieces share a commitment: to the importance of curiosity, to the value of noticing, to the language of politics ('liberty . . . is connected with prose'), to the political intelligence of the arts, and – perhaps above all – to the importance of being decent. Here was an individual who was able to formulate views that were the product of humility, clear-sightedness, generosity, honesty, humour, sanity (Isherwood remarked that Forster was 'saner than anyone else I know'), and who was determined to articulate them at a time when many other writers and intellectuals were either silent about, or complicit with, the threat of National Socialism. Certain of these qualities could, of course, be found in his fiction, but here they were present in a more emphatic way.

In the first of 'Three Anti-Nazi Broadcasts', for example, he tackles the idea, much discussed at the time, that National Socialism was about purification, was a 'revolution of the soul'. 'This sounds all right,' he replies, 'but why does the soul always require a machine-gun?' Elsewhere he concedes that 'Tolerance is a very dull virtue', but notes that it is all that we have to build a civil society; and when he finds tolerance threatened or weakened by belief, he opens an essay on the subject ('What I Believe') by stating: 'I do not believe in belief. But this is an age of faith, and there are so many militant creeds that, in self-defence, one has to formulate a creed of one's own.' In the same piece, democracy is to be praised because it does not tend to produce 'that unmanageable type of citizen known as the Great man'. In his place, 'It produces instead different kinds of small men – a much finer achievement.'

Forster liked to call such people his aristocrats, by which he meant those who could be numbered among 'the sensitive, the considerate and the plucky', and whom he characterized more expansively as follows:

They are sensitive for others as well as for themselves, they are considerate without being fussy, their pluck is not swankiness but the power to endure, and they can take a joke. I give no examples – it is risky to do that – but the reader may as well consider whether this is the type of person he would like to meet and to be . . .

It is not just the sentiments that are appealing here, but the temperament from which they flow. 'He's strong because he doesn't try to be a stiff-lipped stoic like the rest of us, and so he'll never crack,' said Isherwood, and it was that sense of his strength that appealed to me; that, and Forster's related commitment to the value of the modest, the everyday, the small, the seemingly negligible. Size – a sense of proportion and decorum – was important to him, and his example shows why it should be important to us, too; how it can help *us* to register the glory of the ordinary, the imperfect, the compromised. 'No one can spend his or her life entirely in the creation or the appreciation of masterpieces,' he writes in 'Art for Art's Sake', and time after time in this collection we are encouraged to consider the importance of looking elsewhere and everywhere, and at the things we cannot do or have not done.

In the elegiac piece that concludes *Two Cheers for Democracy*, 'The Last of Abinger', Forster presents us with some extracts from a diary that reveal his deep affection for place, his sensitivity to the beauties of the turning world and his sense of its sadness. In this lovely meditation, he searches for meaning in the English countryside; resolves to learn the names of all the fields in the parish; wishes he had talked more to old men; writes of how his heart beats to the importance of nature; swiftly wonders if it is proper to feel that way; records being visited by 'the sense of a world that asks to be noticed rather than explained'. It is a sense that fills the pages of this extraordinary volume: a book that is itself sensitive, considerate, plucky, and that stands as the record of a figure who was able to face a world that was tragic without becoming tragic himself.

MATTHEW ADAMS *is a recovering academic and a freelance writer. He is working on his first novel.*

Social Climbing Is Risky

ALEXANDER LUCIE-SMITH

When my old English master died, I was lucky enough to have the first pick of his library. Most of the standard works of English Literature were there, including many beautiful old Oxford University Press editions, all bearing the signs of much use, and annotations in his instantly recognizable handwriting. Because JFM (as we called him) had taught me to love literature – I was young then, and how I wish I had listened more, and learned more! – I feel now, as I turn the pages that he once read, and look up quotations where he once searched, that he is teaching me still.

Like all enthusiastic readers, he had his favourites (Jane Austen, for example) as well as those whom he politely but firmly termed 'overrated', such as D. H. Lawrence. Among his books I found, as expected, no Lawrence, though I did come across (and instantly commandeered) the complete works of Graham Greene. He had never mentioned Greene: perhaps, as a strict Catholic, he thought him a touch too heretical for Catholic schoolboys.

I took books that I knew would be useful, and so they have proved. And almost as an afterthought I took three old Faber paperbacks – L. P. Hartley's Eustace and Hilda trilogy: *The Shrimp and the Anemone*, *The Sixth Heaven* and *Eustace and Hilda*. I was conscious that this was unfashionable literature, but thought the books might

---

L. P. Hartley, *The Shrimp and the Anemone* (1944), *The Sixth Heaven* (1946) and *Eustace and Hilda* (1947) are available in a single volume, introduced by Anita Brookner: New York Review of Books · Pb · 876pp · £17.61 · ISBN 9780940322806.

tell me more about JFM's reading tastes. He had never mentioned them; perhaps they were another secret enthusiasm.

Naturally, I knew of L. P. Hartley; many of my contemporaries had had to 'do' *The Go-Between* for O level. I had read this later book – published in 1953 – and seen the film, but we never 'did' it in class, and I can now see why. JFM wanted us to think for ourselves. *The Go-Between* is not dull, but it is formulaic, heavy with symbols, inviting stock responses. JFM did not believe in 'set answers' or in rote learning. So I wondered why this trilogy was on his shelves. It's a question I've only recently answered. For a decade and a half I've been carrying the paperbacks with me from house to house, but only now have I got round to reading them.

The trilogy's central characters are a pair of siblings, Eustace and Hilda. The story spans the First World War, beginning with Eustace

Mary Kuper

as a little boy and ending with him in early manhood. The children's mother is dead, and by the opening of the second volume, so is their father. Eustace is the novels' centre of consciousness; Hilda, who is four years older, is seen through his eyes; his vision is what the novels are about. As you might expect from a skilled writer, Eustace's vision is flawed: the reader often sees more than he does.

When the trilogy opens the pair are living in Norfolk, at the seaside, members of the straitened middle class. The household keeps no carriage, and Eustace is not destined to go to a public school; there is a servant, but the house is small. Family life is claustrophobic, presided over by a maiden aunt. Then things change. An old lady in a bath chair, whom Eustace at first sees as an ogress, takes an interest in him; Hilda insists he go to tea with this Miss Fothergill; the two become friends and play piquet together. When Miss Fothergill dies she leaves Eustace £18,000. This means he can now become a gentleman; his father accepts the legacy, against the advice of the aunt.

Around this time Eustace falls ill during a paperchase and is taken to Anchorstone Hall, the local great house, where he meets Dick Stavely, 15 years old, handsome, kind, charming and aristocratic. Eustace likes Dick, but Dick is attracted to Hilda, and much as Eustace dreams of being invited back to the Hall, it is Hilda, not Eustace, Dick wants to see, though Hilda is not at all interested. However, now that Eustace has money, he is surely closer to Dick's social milieu.

And so it proves in the second volume, when Eustace, now an undergraduate, makes it to the Hall, along with his sister, who has become a rather severe bluestocking. He has shared his inheritance with her, and she is using it for charitable purposes. Dick pursues Hilda without apparent success and, perhaps unwittingly, charms Eustace. Eustace is using Hilda to secure his position with Dick, and the Stavely family are not pleased at the prospect of Dick marrying a middle-class girl. At this point Dick's aunt, Lady Nelly, invites Eustace to her Venetian palazzo for the summer in order, we later discover, to remove him so that the family can effectively scotch Dick's relationship with Hilda.

The third volume is set in Venice, with Hilda and Dick's romance off-stage in England. I won't reveal what happens, but only say that the triangular relationship and the manipulations are handled with great subtlety. The importance of money, and the fact that love is not quite all it seems, are reminiscent of Henry James. Eustace is an innocent caught in the toils. So is Hilda, though she is less innocent, more knowing, though what she knows we do not ever quite discover. Hartley is at home with these Jamesian themes, and he has a lightness of touch that the Master often lacks.

Two forces are at work here and throughout the trilogy, both beloved of the English novelist: sex and snobbery. Eustace is a social climber, though a naïve one, and his legacy enables him to rise; but it is not really enough to enable him to rise definitively. He doesn't enjoy the unquestioned status of, say, the heiress Isabel Archer in *The Portrait of a Lady*. Eustace's legacy is enough to give him a taste for the high life without giving him the means to satisfy that taste completely. So, staying in the Venetian palazzo with Lady Nelly, he is an outsider, an oddity, though he seems unaware of it.

Eustace is also sexually naïve. There is no hint that he finds Dick sexually attractive, though it is hinted that Dick might be interested in him (after all Dick was at Harrow, and might well be au fait with homosexuality in a way middle-class Eustace is not). But Eustace is more than simply virginal; he seems asexual; in Venice a childhood friend, now a rather racy divorcée, tries to pick him up, and he comically misreads the signals. Sex means nothing to him; he seems unaware of the almost absurdly flirtatious gondoliers Lady Nelly employs, or the significance of her Italian lover. All this, perhaps, points to something greater: he is a spectator at the game of life, an onlooker, not a participant.

Hilda is less keen to succeed socially than her brother, but as a woman she has to fend off male sexual advances, which she does with disastrous ineptitude. The siblings have a younger sister who is married at 18, and who says of Hilda: 'She doesn't understand men, and has never tried to.' Why Hilda should be so frigid is never explained. There is no hint that she is attracted to her own sex, but it is clear that she fears and loathes men. Despite her beauty and intelligence, she remains a social misfit.

The aunt has this to say: 'No good ever comes of trying to climb out of the class of society into which you are born . . . Eustace always had a hankering after rich people, and it will be his undoing, just as he has made it Hilda's. He goes about with them, but he does not understand their way of looking at things, nor did Hilda.' In the end it may be better to stay in one's own familiar milieu, dull as that may be, than to try and break out of confinement. Freedom can be terrifying.

The Eustace and Hilda trilogy is a comedy of manners, an illustration of how the middle classes are lost in the upper-class world of great houses and Venetian palazzi, and puzzled by men called Dick who do not share their bourgeois morality. But like all good comedy, it has an underlying seriousness. The world Eustace finds himself in is mysterious to him; for his sister, who is more perspicacious, it is frightening. And how true this still rings, several decades later: some of us find life socially awkward, or are not quite at ease in our own skins sexually – or both.

A reissue twelve years ago by the *New York Review of Books* described the trilogy as 'a comedy of upper-class manners; a study in the subtlest nuances of feeling; a poignant reckoning with the ironies of character and fate . . . about the ties that bind'. Yes, but it is more than that: it becomes darker as it progresses, darkest of all in the sunlit Venetian scenes, though this darkness is always subtle.

The *NYRB* edition also quotes Betjeman's judgement: 'The combined effect of these three books is one of mounting excellence. Eustace, the central figure, is an immortal portrayal of the delights and agonies of childhood and adolescence.' The truth is that Eustace never grows up, and it is in this that the trilogy's greatness lies: it is a simple and beguiling story, but under its polished surface lurk truths that perhaps we would rather not face.

ALEXANDER LUCIE-SMITH is a Catholic priest who writes on cultural matters.

The Plots Thicken

RICHARD PLATT

On New Year's Eve 2013 I was standing in the kitchen of a house overlooking the Pacific Ocean in California, chatting to an Englishman who writes English subtitles for French films. We began to talk about *Beowulf,* David and Goliath, and *Jaws.* Then one of us said, with a shrug and an upward sweep of the hands, 'They're the same story.' The other nodded. A flash of recognition passed between us which said, 'You've read *that* book too?' And indeed we had.

It has become something of a truism in literary circles, since at least the middle of the eighteenth century, that all the world's literature, and indeed all the world's storytelling, can be reduced to a handful of storylines. Goethe believed this, as did Samuel Johnson, who contemplated writing a book on this theme but gave it up.

Fortunately, another man did not give up. He took all the world's storytelling from the *Epic of Gilgamesh* to *Star Wars* – myth, legend, films, novels, theatre, opera, narrative poetry, everything and everyone, from Dante to Tolkien, Homer to Hemingway – and boiled it down to seven basic plots. It took him more than thirty years. It is a wonder it did not take him thirty decades.

The result is 700 pages of not-terribly-large print which read like an adventure story. I passed the book on to a friend, an accomplished actor who fell in love with theatre because he loves storytelling, and it destroyed his life for a week. His wife couldn't get him off the sofa.

Christopher Booker, *The Seven Basic Plots: Why We Tell Stories* (2004)
Continuum · Pb · 736pp · £17.99 · ISBN 9780826480378

The man who accomplished this thirteenth labour of Hercules, this literary distillation that forges friendships and threatens marriages, is Christopher Booker, and his book is *The Seven Basic Plots: Why We Tell Stories* (2004).

Known to British readers as the founding editor of *Private Eye* and a contributor to the *Sunday Telegraph*, Booker has written a stout pile of books, none of which, I must confess, I have read, though their titles would suggest he thinks for himself, does not shun controversy and, armed with a satiric wit, relishes being contrary. Good for him. The world needs more contrarians, if only to keep the rest of us intellectually honest and clear in our thinking. And he seems to have ruffled more than a few feathers. No matter. He wrote *The Seven Basic Plots*, and that's good enough for me.

Booker has that peculiar genius which connects commonplaces that we would never have connected for ourselves, makes observations that, only when once made, are self-evident, and asks questions we would never have thought to ask. The world's greatest storytellers are among the most famous and honoured people in history. Why? What is the value of storytelling? What need does it fulfil? Why is storytelling central to our humanity? Why is it that some stories are inherently satisfying, even spiritually nourishing, while others leave us with an empty or incomplete feeling? What is the role of numbers in storytelling? Why is it that there are few things as compelling in storytelling as the desire to have the threads of narrative untangled and explained? These are the questions Booker sets out to answer. It is a task that would have brought a lesser man to despair.

He begins with the basic structure of story, organizing plotlines by commonalities which are sometimes self-evident and at other times surprising. His Seven Basic Plots are: Overcoming the Monster (*Beowulf, Jaws*), Rags to Riches (*Aladdin, Oliver Twist*), The Quest (Homer's *Odyssey, Watership Down*), Comedy (Aristophanes, The Marx Brothers), Tragedy (*Oedipus, Macbeth*), Rebirth (*Sleeping Beauty, A Christmas Carol*) and Voyage and Return (*Peter Rabbit,*

Brideshead Revisited). (One wonders what Evelyn Waugh would have made of that last pairing.) Booker points out that there are very few works that interweave all seven basic plots, but one that does is a twentieth-century masterpiece. It will surprise no one who has read it to learn that this work is *The Lord of the Rings*.

Booker also finds archetypal figures inhabiting the world of story, each with its evil twin or 'dark inversion', all of whom interact to create the masculine-feminine, good-and-evil tension that makes the machinery turn: the Wise Old Man, the Good King and Queen, the Companion, the Child, the Helpful Animal, the Trickster and the Other Half, who must unite with the hero or heroine to make them whole. Booker concludes that

> the real significance of our ability to tell stories is twofold. Firstly, it provides a uniquely revealing mirror to the dynamics of human nature. But secondly, by laying bare the unconscious foundations which underlie so much of the way we view the world, this can in turn cast an extraordinarily revealing light on . . . almost every aspect of human thought and behaviour.

And he is not content to stop there. He now proceeds to lay bare those unconscious foundations. He notices that after 5,000 years of storytelling, something in the last 200 years has changed. Storytelling has broken free of its archetypal mooring and been set adrift. The storyteller is no longer an adventurer sailing from port with sails unfurled, but a rudderless wanderer without hope of landfall.

Booker turns to Yeats to voice his darkest forebodings:

> Things fall apart; the centre cannot hold;
> Mere anarchy is loosed upon the world,
> The blood-dimmed tide is loosed, and everywhere
> The ceremony of innocence is drowned;
> The best lack all conviction, while the worst
> Are full of passionate intensity.

Having watched others hold the mirror up to life, he now holds life up to the mirror. He turns his attention from storytelling outward, to the storytellers and to the societies that produce them, and asks what has unloosed Yeats's rising blood-dimmed tide that, as Booker sees it, has debauched storytelling since the Romantic period.

What he finds is that the emerging creative impulse is, as Wordsworth wrote of Shelley's poetry,

> what astrology is to natural science . . . a confused embodying of vague abstraction – a fever of the soul, thirsting and craving after what it cannot have, indulging its love of power and novelty at the expense of truth and nature.

Booker is deliciously, bracingly opinionated, and is not afraid to play the iconoclast. His perspective is grounded in Jungian psychology. Thus he believes that the purpose of story is to help us see what it means to be a healthy, whole and wholly integrated human being, our emotions, intellect, senses and intuition united in the four archetypal attributes of personhood: strength, order, compassion and understanding. These attributes are designed to counterbalance one another. When they are thrown into conflict, the centre cannot hold. Stories light the way through the labyrinth in which the journey of personal growth takes place, and the false pathways in which we lose ourselves.

What Booker detects in the modern artistic ethos, not merely in literature but also in theatre, music and art, is a bedlam of egocentricity. The orientation is turned inward, where strength, order, compassion and understanding have no communal context, leaving the artist blind, stunted and barren, the degradation of storytelling reaching its nadir in the hopeless futility of Beckett, Chekhov, Proust, Joyce. It would be virtually impossible for all of his observations and conclusions to be right, for even a man with his genius cannot be expected flawlessly to accomplish the task he has set himself, yet he is extremely convincing, and in those rare moments where he is unconvincing, he is always challenging, and writes with a narrative grace that is seldom seen in work of this scholarly calibre.

There is an in-depth case study of Thomas Hardy which was for me particularly gratifying, as I have always found Hardy's invincible pessimism hard going, and when I finished Booker's analysis of *Ulysses*, which he says is 'inspired' by Homer's *Odyssey* only in the sense that it is a revoltingly vulgar comic strip parody, I gave away my copy of Joyce. Booker was right. I no longer wanted Joyce sullying my shelves. To read Booker is to be forever transformed, almost cleansed, as a reader.

Having disentangled the narrative strands of millennia, Booker then intertwines them into one universal, perfect plot; one plot that explains all storytelling; one plot that is so inherently satisfying, so essential to human nature, so nourishing, so central to our growth and health, so foundational to our humanity, that no effective story-telling can ignore it. And that plot is . . .

But I will leave this for Mr Booker to explain.

RICHARD PLATT is the author of *As One Devil to Another*, a fiendish correspondence in the tradition of C. S. Lewis's *The Screwtape Letters*. He is currently plotting a new novel, *The Forest of Nede*, also inspired by the works of Lewis: www.RichardPlattAuthor.com.

O'Brian's World

GRANT MCINTYRE

This is the third and last part of a short sequence on Patrick O'Brian's twenty naval novels. 'A Friendship of Opposites' (in Issue 40) was about Jack Aubrey and Stephen Maturin, two great originals of twentieth-century fiction, and how they draw us not just into the warfare of wooden ships but into the whole Georgian era, which O'Brian makes as fresh as if we were part of it, living in the midst of its chaos and energy, experiencing its harshness, courtesy, relentlessness, absurdity and the rest. 'The House that Jack Built' (in Issue 42) turned to the two men's marriages, which are easily as compelling – affectionate, complicated, believable relationships, full of misunderstanding and comedy as much as of love. It also touched on Jack's other great love, the Navy, which for him is almost the staff of life despite its radical flaws – most the result of folly and greed – and its casual cruelty. This last piece is about a different sort of relationship, that of the author and his subject. It's largely about Stephen, because when O'Brian drew Stephen he had one eye on himself.

Patrick O'Brian's Aubrey/Maturin novels comprise: *Master and Commander* (1969); *Post Captain* (1972); *HMS Surprise* (1973); *The Mauritius Command* (1977); *Desolation Island* (1978); *The Fortune of War* (1979); *The Surgeon's Mate* (1980); *The Ionian Mission* (1981); *Treason's Harbour* (1983); *The Far Side of the World* (1984); *The Reverse of the Medal* (1986); *The Letter of Marque* (1988); *The Thirteen-Gun Salute* (1989); *The Nutmeg of Consolation* (1991); *Clarissa Oakes* (1992); *The Wine-Dark Sea* (1993); *The Commodore* (1994); *The Yellow Admiral* (1996); *The Hundred Days* (1998); *Blue at the Mizzen* (1999); and *The Final Unfinished Voyage of Jack Aubrey* (2004). All are available as paperbacks from HarperCollins.

Everyone who knew O'Brian spotted at once that he and Stephen Maturin appeared to be very alike – both outsiders, both odd-looking, learned, extremely reticent men who were not what they seemed. But in reality it was the likeness that was not what it seemed. Stephen's reticence concealed feats of espionage, cryptography, black propaganda, political intrigue and sudden violence, O'Brian's that sadly he couldn't lay claim to anything in that line. He might well have been very effective but he was never given the chance he wanted, even during the War. So he didn't, as some authors do, put himself into his books, he put his invented self into them. He liked to suggest that he'd sailed in a square-rigged three-master, but it seems he never did, nor did he experience the seas he described so dazzlingly well. He did live for years in Collioure, so he knew Catalonia, but on the other hand there was nothing Irish about him at all – he hardly went there. He was not even Patrick O'Brian before he chose to be. His early life as Patrick Russ was so disastrous he ruthlessly put it behind him, and almost came to believe in the past he would rather have had.

O'Brian certainly was like Stephen, though, in the range of his knowledge. It's amazing to read that he spent only three years at school, and otherwise was largely self-taught, because one of the qualities that make his novels such a pleasure is the deep but unassertive erudition that runs through them. It's not just that his naval operations are generally based on fact (with Jack often in the role of Lord Cochrane) or that historical admirals appear absolutely in person, it's more that O'Brian has a complete sense of his period in all its aspects. Every detail can be trusted, though none is ever put on obvious display. He knows everything about the construction of ships and their handling, and also about naval notions of honour, which at that time were shadowed by sloth, corruption and greed. He knows about uniforms of course, but also about ball gowns and what they say about their wearers. He's very good on minor religious sects like the Sethians or the Knipperdollings and their modestly self-righteous bearing which masks all the usual sins. Likewise he has an exact sense of musical taste in those not quite at the cutting edge; or of superstition on the lower decks (and the quarterdeck too); or prejudices and hypocrisies among the gentry – or equally among the prostitutes, swindlers and hard cases of the underclass. Naturally he's good on eighteenth-century science and medicine, and on how knowledge was achieved. Here is Stephen advising a younger man he's taken under his wing:

> More than any book I do most earnestly recommend a private corpse. Your school cadaver, tossed about in wanton play, your odd heads and parts indifferently picked by the porter's wife, are well enough for the coarse processes; but for the fine work, give me a good fresh private corpse, preferably a pauper, to avoid the fat.

O'Brian's mastery of language is most wonderful of all. He manages to capture that mixture of toughness and grace which, for me at least, makes formal eighteenth-century English so attractive. Also the verbal violence that makes demotic eighteenth-century English so vivid. He catches Stephen's subtle Irishness, or the slightly un-idiomatic English of highly educated South Americans, or the competitiveness of children, or the way one wife can make her opinion of another very clear without expressing it, or Jack can make his authority absolute without disrespect – and he does it all in the language of the time. 'He catches it all flawlessly. Yes, you think, reading the witty, textured exchanges. This is surely what they were like.' That's from Charlton Heston (I was surprised too). There is never the least visible strain; one never feels his characters are putting on a historical act, but always that they are revealing themselves, unknowingly, in everything they say.

None of this erudition interferes with the storytelling. It's true there are plenty of naval battles from which it's hardly possible to look away, and plenty of danger on land too, even in a balloon. But O'Brian's narrative skill propels scenes of every kind. When Jack's malevolent mother-in-law proposes to intervene in Stephen's upbringing of his damaged daughter (her great-niece), their dialogue almost makes the page vibrate. The court case where Jack is accused of defrauding the Stock Exchange, believes that his innocence will protect him and comes to see that it won't, is completely compelling in a quite different way. Incidentally, O'Brian's stepson Nikolai Tolstoy believed this episode had its origin in his own – Tolstoy's – libel battle with Lord Aldington. They had similarly happy outcomes too, in the end.

The storytelling is enhanced by O'Brian's extraordinary inventiveness. Confining examples to Stephen alone: we find him at a levée, with sycophants like flies around the Duke of Clarence; or in a kind of animal Shangri-La where he is shown around by an elderly orang-utan, who takes a dim view of the morals of other apes. We see him sneak a look from a high cell in the Temple Prison towards a window in the wonderfully named rue des Neuf Fiancées, where there's a pretty widow who may help with escape if she fancies his younger companion; or in the high Andes in a storm of unbreathable powdered snow, protected only by a dead llama. Here he is on board ship, following a hurricane:

> The *Boadicea* was lying to under a scrap of mizzen staysail, riding the tremendous seas nobly, shouldering them aside with her bluff bows: her fore and main topmasts had gone by the board; wild ropes by the score stretched horizontally aft from the wrecked tops, sometimes cracking as loud as a gun; her remain-

ing shrouds were packed with scraps of terrestrial vegetation – a palm-frond was clearly recognizable. But this was not the curious sight. From the drowned forecastle aft, and particularly on the quarterdeck, wherever there was the slightest lee, there were birds. Seabirds for the most part but right by him a little creature like a thrush. It did not move as he approached it, nor even when he touched its back. The others were the same, and he looked into the lustrous eye of a bosun bird from within a few inches.

O'Brian's inventiveness extends to his characters as much as to incident, and his characters naturally age and grow more substantial as we get to know them better. What a shame it would be never to meet small, priapic William Babbington, who first appears as a piping midshipman and in the end commands his own small ship; or Preserved Killick, Jack's sour, shrewish, devoted steward, always on hand to overhear sensitive conversations in the captain's cabin and pass them round the ship's company; or the naked and scrawny little Melanesian twins Lucy and Emily – 'so plain, poor things' – rescued from an island devastated by smallpox. They jointly become Stephen's loblolly boy, cleaning up blood, slime and body parts in his surgery, and learning seamen's and officers' English as two different languages. They eventually become Londoners and add cockney too. And there is Sam, who provokes smiles whenever he appears because he's the spitting image of Jack – is so obviously his son from an early fling – despite being black and still more incongruously a priest, making his way up the Roman Catholic hierarchy.

All these characters are portrayed in the round, with an inner life and a life off the page that one can easily imagine. O'Brian writes all their parts with humour – the sometimes serious humour of comic opera. He looks on them with clear-sighted generosity and understanding, so one can grasp the fears and uncertainties of even the worst. In fact one can see oneself in them quite often, in a world which A. S. Byatt said 'is our own but not our own'. It's not escapist but curiously encouraging to read of others coping in such different circumstances, and not always competently, with some of what we have to cope with too. It's helpful that they suffer, as occasionally we all do in life, from a shocking disconnect between deserts and rewards – the way fate or arbitrary power can deliver undeserved happiness or undeserved tragedy.

And just in case it's the second, we can always keep by us these lines of cod Pope, written by a sailor poet called James Mowett who comes second in a mid-ocean poetry sweepstake:

> Even calamity, by thought refined,
> Inspirits and adorns the thinking mind.

GRANT MCINTYRE has worked with books and with sculpture, but is all at sea when it comes to ships.

A Salute to Betjeman

RANJIT BOLT

On Hampstead Heath a leisured stroll
To calm the mind and soothe the soul –
North London's take on Flatford Mill –
The air is thick with heat, and still,
The sunshine gilds the two hilltops
Burnishes meadow, pond and copse.
All round a gorgeous vista spreads
Though (adders lurk in all woodsheds)
The TV mast on Highgate Hill's
A blot; the Royal Free – bitter pills
For anyone who cares, to swallow
And doubtless, some day, worse will follow
As Betjeman once prophesied
While all around him beauty died.
   I sit beneath a spreading oak
In whose wide shade Jack Straw once spoke
(Or might have) to the multitude
As nation-changing trouble brewed,
And fish out from my bag the book
That, in unheedful haste, I took
Along with me today. I scan
The cover – find it's . . . Betjeman!
The self-same legendary lamenter

John Betjeman, *Collected Poems* (2006)
John Murray · Pb · 528pp · £14.99 · ISBN 9780719568503

Of parking lot and shopping centre,
Church wrecking-balled and hedgerow felled
On whom my thoughts have briefly dwelled
Already. 'Christ!' I think, 'not him!
All old-style rhyme and meter – grim!'
    At once 'A Bay in Anglesey'
With its sure grip on prosody
And masterly descriptive power
Painterly in its image shower
Disarms my modernist prejudice –
No mere hack rhymester writes like this:
The sleepy sound of a tea-time tide
Slaps at the rocks the sun has dried
Too lazy, almost, to sink and lift
Round low peninsulas pink with thrift.
A poet needs no more to speak
In his defence than a technique
That Tennyson would not have scorned.
    In more than half his work he warned
Of ineluctable decline
And kicked against the pricks of Time,
Conservative defines his views,
Nostalgia's, as it were, his muse.
But his brave railing at decay
And longing for a bygone day
Speak loud to us, leap off the page
In this jejune and tasteless age.
If all nostalgia has been banned
For England's green and pleasant land
Still 'Slough' presents us something true,
What Pope said poetry should do –
Express, that is, 'what oft was thought',
A common feeling neatly caught,

It's not their fault they do not know
The birdsong from the radio,
It's not their fault they often go
To Maidenhead.

Snobbish, and yet we side with him
And go out with him on his limb:
'Encase your Legs in nylons' sings
Of equally depressing things
And, in the same dark vein, decries
Taste's, beauty's, hastening demise:
Encase your legs in nylons,
Bestride your hills with pylons
O age without a soul;
Away with gentle willows
And all the elmy billows
That through your valleys roll.
This dwelling on lost sights and times –
Reactionary, and yet it chimes
When I look up and, with a chill,
See that mast marring Highgate Hill
And, in retreat from philistines
And Nokia's dastardly designs,
St Michael's now beleaguered spire
Pricking the bums of the heavenly choir.
  One of the poet's chief regrets
Was having missed his share of sex.
His Surrey subaltern's love song,
Famously, hits us with a strong
Aroma of testosterone
(Apparently the poet's own).*

---

* The subject of the poem, Joan Jackson, née Hunter Dunn, was, as is well
  documented, an acquaintance of Betjeman, who fell in love with her, com-

What literate, lusty male's not yearned
To have his tennis serve returned
By his own Miss Joan Hunter Dunn?
Lord Alfred would have chalked this one
Up on his list of twenty best
And it sails through the Kipling test.
Here's proof that writing from the heart
Can still be consonant with art:
Her father's euonymus shines as we walk,
And swing past the summer-house, buried in talk,
And cool the veranda that welcomes us in
To the six-o'clock news and a lime-juice and gin . . .
The Hillman is waiting, the light's in the hall
The pictures of Egypt are bright on the wall.
With masterly economy
A few sharp details let us see
A typical Home Counties scene
While sex, as the implicit theme,
Is handled with an attitude
That's neither innocent nor crude
And details accurate as a laser:
A mere discarded shorts and blazer,
The bubbling of a bath being run
By the delectable Miss Dunn
Are filled with an erotic charge
Here is the girl next door writ large.
Then there's that winsome tone – aloof,
Amused, detached, yet not quite proof
Against the charms of Aldershot,
Bourgeois, conventional, or not.

posing in her honour 'A Subaltern's Love Song', in which he fantasizes about
their engagement.

So, flimsy though he sometimes seems,
He does attack the larger themes,
Nor is he always frivolous
Or quite insouciant when he does.
After a terrible review
He thinks of suicide, but in lieu
Uses 'Tregardock' to work out,
With great aplomb, angst, gloom, self-doubt:
And I, on my volcano edge,
Exposed to ridicule and hate
Still do not dare to leap the ledge
And smash to pieces on the slate.
    In 'Death in Leamington' this gloom
Is present in the lonely room
Where an old lady dies alone –
An easy mastery of tone,
That eye for detail and, again,
Rhythmically, Kipling's influence plain:
She bolted the big round window,
She let the blinds unroll,
She set a match to the mantle,
She covered the fire with coal.
That's not the Betjeman the slick
Modernist critics love to kick,
All tea and scones and porticoes,
But it is poetry, not prose
Chopped into bits and written down
In stanzas by some skill-less clown.
Betjeman asks: what's wrong with *form?*
Slack, shapeless tripe may be the norm
In these none-too-poetic times
When poets shun meter, spit on rhymes
Maintaining there's no substance to them

When actually they just can't do them,
But, notwithstanding, discipline
Was never, isn't now, a sin.
    I recall having little time
For Betjeman in my fiery prime.
He'd read his poems on TV
Or radio, and it would be
At him, not with him, that I laughed
But now I can admire his craft,
Conceding that in naked skill
There lies huge merit. And I still,
After that Hampstead afternoon –
Like hearing someone sing in tune
After a droning rapper loon –
Will put aside some fool collection
And choose Sir John for an injection
Of wit, sheer competence, panache –
Something, in short, that we'd be rash
To overlook, and ought to treasure:
Poetry one can read *for pleasure.*

RANJIT BOLT was born in Manchester in 1959 of Anglo-Indian parentage. His translations and adaptations of foreign classic plays have been performed in major theatres all over the English-speaking world, including the National Theatre and the Royal Shakespeare Company.
    The illustrations in this article are by Daniel Macklin.

Pastures of the Sky

LINDA LEATHERBARROW

It's easy to imagine yourself treading in the footprints of a famous writer, we're encouraged to do so all the time – those blue plaques, those National Trust signs – but it's altogether a different experience when you find yourself, as I did one evening on the corner of Lexington Avenue in New York, having a shivery goosebump moment, not with a well-known author, but with his fictional character: Holly Golightly.

One of those brownstones, I thought, with a fire escape at the back, that modest bar where she would have gone to make telephone calls and pick up her messages, that yellow cab . . . then there she was, swishing elegantly past in a little black dress, matching elbow-length gloves, and a string of pearls round her neck. Only, of course, I realized a moment later that this wasn't the 'real' Holly Golightly that Truman Capote had so magnificently created in his 1958 novella, *Breakfast at Tiffany's*, but a twenty-first-century girl wearing a fashionably retro dress and off to a party or a date. A discombobulating moment, though a peculiarly appropriate one as the 'real' Holly is continually re-making her image and social identity.

She belongs, however, in the 1940s, when America was still at war and opportunities for women to pursue careers or gain financial independence were limited. 'Be good, sweet maid, and let who will be clever,' my father used to instruct me, even in the 'liberated' 1960s. Holly is neither good nor sweet, but she *is* clever, and charming, part

Truman Capote, *Breakfast at Tiffany's* (1958)
Penguin · Pb · 160pp · £8.99 · ISBN 9780141182797

rôle model, part anti-heroine, her character firmly underpinned by Capote's deep understanding of the psychology of aspiration and desire.

He began life as Truman Streckfus Persons. His parents divorced when he was 4 and left him in the care of his mother's hard-up relatives in Monroeville, Alabama. Four years later he was reunited with his mother, Lillie Mae Faulk, who had acquired a second husband, a New York textile broker, Joseph Capote. Truman acquired a new name, Truman Garcia Capote. Unfortunately, his stepfather was convicted of embezzlement and the family home on Park Avenue was lost.

While still a schoolboy, Truman began to write short stories – a few were published – and would blag his way into Manhattan night-clubs such as the Stork Club, frequented by movie stars, celebrities and aristocrats. After leaving school, he worked for *The New Yorker* for two years, cultivated a distinctive high-pitched voice and an off-beat manner, and was open about his sexuality at a time when being actively gay was illegal in the States.

I was 16 when I first read *Breakfast at Tiffany's*, but because this is a novella that begins with an ending, full of uncertainties and possibilities, I soon realized that this was a complex grown-up story in which there might be sadness as well as joy. The unnamed narrator – whom Holly calls Fred because he reminds her of a much-loved younger brother – sees that she is schooled in the dark arts of glamour and seduction yet is intrigued by the reckless bravado of her disclosures. Whatever you do, seems to be her message, do it with style, and ignore convention. 'Leave it to me,' she says. 'I'm always top banana in the shock department.'

Sharing Holly's apartment in that East Seventies brownstone in Manhattan is a striped red cat who also has no name, a stray given strictly temporary accommodation. The narrator moves into a single attic room above them with everything he needs to become a writer: books and jars of pencils to sharpen. But he is quickly distracted; first by the printed card in her mailbox name-slot – *Miss Holiday*

Golightly, Travelling – then by her habit of coming home in the small hours without a door key and expecting one of the other tenants to let her in.

It's late one night that he finally gets to know her better. Lying in bed, unable to sleep and reading a book, he is disturbed by a feeling of being watched. It's Holly standing outside the window, looking in.

'I've got the most terrifying man downstairs,' she said, stepping off the fire escape into the room. 'I mean he's sweet when he isn't drunk, but let him start lapping up the vino, and oh God quel beast!'

Holly, who began life as Lulamae Barnes (her first name a close match to Capote's mother's name), grew up sleeping four to a bed, somewhere unspecified, possibly in rural Oklahoma. She has been fending for herself ever since she ran away from home at 14 and now, at 19, is a shameless gold-digger who lives a superficially glitzy life, hanging out in fashionable nightclubs and restaurants, or throwing impromptu parties at her apartment, still furnished mainly with suitcases and unpacked crates. 'I liked its fly-by-night look,' says the narrator.

He is a little dazzled by Holly, which is hardly surprising as she so often appears draped only in a bath towel or dressed up to the nines. She's ruthlessly ambitious, but at times also touchingly self-aware. This is how she describes Tiffany's, the upmarket jewellery store on Fifth Avenue.

It calms me down right away, the quietness and the proud look of it; nothing very bad could happen to you there, not with those kind men in their nice suits, and that lovely smell of silver and alligator wallets. If I could find a real life place like Tiffany's, then I'd buy some furniture and give the cat a name.

As their friendship grows, the narrator gives Holly a silver St Christopher medal (the patron saint of travellers) because it's all he can afford at Tiffany's and she gives him an empty birdcage, an elaborate bamboo palace, that he has spotted in an antique store on 51st Street. 'If you let yourself love a wild thing,' she says later on, and a little drunk, 'you'll end up looking at the sky.'

The narrator is not the only one who ends up looking at the sky. There are many others, including Salvatore 'Sally' Tomato, the dope racketeer in Sing Sing prison whom Holly visits every Thursday in order to pass on a mysterious 'weather report', which turns out to be code for something very different; O. J. Berman, a Hollywood actor's agent who arranged French and English lessons for Holly when she was just 15, hoping the right voice would launch a film career; José Ybarra-Jaegar, a Brazilian millionaire who does something 'vaguely important' in Washington; and Doc Golightly, the Texas farmer Holly first married then abandoned. '*Divorce* him? Of course I never divorced him. I was only fourteen, for God's sake. It couldn't have been *legal*.'

Most people don't have her measure, but the reader does, being clued in early on by the obliging O. J. Berman.

'You're wrong. She is a phony. But on the other hand you're right. She isn't a phony because she's a *real* phony. She believes all this crap she believes.'

'Writing has laws of perspective,' Capote told *Paris Review*, 'light and shade, just as painting does, or music.' No one understood this better. His novella is like a house in summer, filled with air, and every object, every character, has a purpose. The red cat, for instance, who is tossed about and disregarded by Holly throughout the story, provides the reader with a dash of comforting sweetness at the very end, necessary because Holly, it turns out, while clever, is not quite clever enough.

Of all his fictional characters, Capote acknowledged that Holly was his favourite and the one most like himself. He, too, liked to travel and lived for a time in Greece, Italy, Africa and the West Indies.

He wrote hugely successful books, both fiction and non-fiction, short stories, plays, film scripts and a musical, but he never seemed fully to shake off the unhappiness of his early life. He drank heavily, took many different drugs and, in the decade leading up to his death in 1984, was in and out of rehab clinics and hospitals.

There is a description of Holly sitting on the fire escape, drying her newly washed hair in the sun, singing and playing her guitar. She knew all the latest show hits but sometimes sang songs with words that suggested the woods and prairies of her childhood home. 'Don't wanna sleep, don't wanna die, just wanna go a-travellin' through the pastures of the sky.' A tune she would play over and over, long after her hair was dry and the lights came on in the city.

LINDA LEATHERBARROW is still writing short stories and lives in Scotland, close to the Galloway Forest Park, the UK's first Dark Sky Park.

Far from a Fling

ROGER HUDSON

The shelves of John Murray seemed filled with books by its strong-minded, often indomitable women writers when I went to work there in 1972: Jane Austen, Queen Victoria, travellers like Isabella Bird, Freya Stark and Dervla Murphy. Elizabeth Grant was one of whom I had not heard; idle curiosity drew me to her but I was soon engrossed. Born in 1797 she died in 1885, her posthumous fame beginning with the publication of her memoirs, edited by her niece (also Lytton Strachey's mother) in 1898. The *Memoirs of a Highland Lady* went through four printings that year and has been reprinted regularly ever since, for readers are fascinated by its picture of the life of a Highland laird's family in the twilight years of the clan system, at Rothiemurchus, the beautiful 'Gateway to the Cairngorms' near Aviemore. Adding to the interest are the casual though then unexceptional cruelties of her upbringing, a mysterious tale of star-crossed love and the eventual ruin of the family fortunes brought about by the political pretensions and financial incompetence of her father.

The memoirs were written between 1845 and 1854, but both before and during these years Elizabeth also kept a diary. In 1980 a selection from this was published as *The Irish Journals of Elizabeth Smith, 1840–50*. Suddenly it was as if a portrait in profile had changed to a

---

Elizabeth Grant's *Memoirs of a Highland Lady* is in print (Canongate · Pb · 720pp · £15 · ISBN 9781841957579), but the edition of her Irish journals, 1840–50, *The Highland Lady in Ireland*, is out of print, as are *A Highland Lady in France, 1843–45*, covering the Smiths' stay there to save money, and *The Highland Lady in Dublin, 1851–6*.

full-face one, and to the girl and young woman on Speyside, in Enlightenment Edinburgh, Regency London and Bombay there had been added the wife of Colonel Smith of Baltiboys in County Wicklow, 14 miles south of Dublin, busy improving their property, before facing the awful famine years from 1845, as one potato crop after another failed.

At Rothiemurchus there was no question of going to a nearby shop for the necessities of life. Instead there were 'such spinnings and weavings, and washings, and dyeings, and churnings, and knittings, and bleachings, and candle-makings, and soap-boilings, and feather cleanings as never are seen or written of in these days'. The house was full of servants and there was a piper who 'declined any work unconnected with whisky, which with plenty of oat-bread and cheese was given to all comers all day long'. Even 'decent gentlewomen began the day with a dram'. The laird might no longer be 'worshipped as a divinity by every human being in the place', but there was still a strong feudal spirit abroad. Entertainment had to be made and it often took the form of dances where 'gentles and simples reeled away in company' or per-formed 'the single and double fling, the shuffle and heel-and-toe step'. The Floaters' Ball, named after those whose job it was to float logs from the surrounding forest down the Spey, was a grand affair with two sets of fiddlers and whisky punch mixed in washtubs.

Mary Kuper

Other aspects of life for the young Elizabeth and her siblings were far from a fling: days beginning with an outdoor plunge in a tub of cold water, 'the ice on the top of which had often to be broken', then dressing in cotton frocks with short sleeves and low necks before a breakfast of bread-and-milk or porridge, both of which she hated. Even when older she still had to get up at 6.30 'without candle or fire or warm water', then practise playing scales for an hour in the dark. If not the piano there was the harp, its strings 'cutting the poor fingers'. Punishments were whippings from her father or being locked in a dark cupboard, or being starved until finally a plate of spinach was eaten well over a day after it had first been refused.

Elizabeth's mother was 'often ailing', her 'habits indolent' and 'she also hated the worry of children'. Her father, 'a man of £12,000 a year' yet not content to look after his estates in Scotland and England, instead went in search of fame, first at the Bar and then in Parliament. Both winning and then losing the notorious rotten borough of Grimsby cost him huge sums of money and by 1820 the family was forced to retreat to the Highlands from Edinburgh. John Peter Grant was given one of the Duke of Bedford's pocket boroughs when he lost Grimsby, so was immune from arrest for debt, but his family's life became increasingly hand-to-mouth. At least without the distractions of city life Elizabeth did much reading and, as she said, 'It was new to me to think.' When finances became really stretched she and her sister Mary tried their hand at writing.

The £40 which their first articles earned was just enough to keep the household afloat, but when the Duke wanted his borough back in 1827, there was nothing for it but for John Peter to leave the country. Luckily for him, there was a very particular favour which he could call in. When George IV had visited Edinburgh in 1822, supplies of his favourite Glenlivet whisky ran out. 'My father sent word to me – I was the cellarer – to empty my pet bin . . . [the whisky from it] and fifty brace of ptarmigan all shot by one man went up to Holyrood House . . . A reminder of this attention at the proper moment . . . ensured to my father [an] Indian judgeship.' John fled first to France, leaving £60,000 of debt behind him. When his family went south to join him for the voyage to Bombay, their coach was seized for an unpaid bill in Edinburgh.

Like so many before and after her, Elizabeth was prostrated by the Indian climate, convinced she only survived the hot weather thanks to supplies of bitter beer, and then appalled at the prospect of four months' wet weather once the monsoon broke. Her uncle, an old India hand, kept telling her to 'wait for Smith', while her cousins assured her he would make a perfect husband, since 'he is so kind to his horses'. When the mysterious Colonel Smith eventually arrived, she soon saw they were right, even though, aged 50, he was eighteen years older than her. They went on honeymoon with an entourage of bullocks and camels and an escort of irregular cavalry, but shortly after, the doctors said the Colonel must return home if his asthma were not to kill him. Luckily his elder brother had died just before the wedding, so he had inherited his 1,200-acre Wicklow estate. They found it in a state of utter neglect, since the brother had been an absentee landlord, with £6,000 of rent in arrears. 'When I first saw it there stood to welcome me a crowd of, as I thought, beggars – dirty queer-looking men doffing their remnants of hats with much civility. "Thim's the tenants", said the only man with a whole coat.'

Kept afloat by the Colonel's army pension and what Elizabeth could make from her writing, they gradually took the estate in hand and rebuilt the ruined big house where their three children were born. Those tenants whose holdings were too small to provide anything like a living were either helped to emigrate or 'furnished with the means of setting up in useful employments, and were fully paid for any value left'. David Thomson, author of those fine memoirs *Nairn in Darkness and Light* and *Woodbrook*, and editor of her *Irish Journals*, took Elizabeth to task over this, and one suspects that it would be hard to find an Irish historian today with much time for her. But a sympathetic reading must make one ask what alternatives were open, short of handing over the land and walking away. She had her blind spots, like her antipathy towards the Catholic priesthood and her continuing suspicion that most emigrants left with money which should have gone to pay rent arrears. She was driven mad by

Irish fecklessness, dishonesty, 'vindictive temper, love of pleasure, undue appreciation of self'. At the same time she could recognize 'the untidy dirt and *fun* of most uncomfortable Ireland', and could write of the Irish that 'as a race they are wonderfully clever people', though she had to add that, 'In this their grub state they are very disheartening to deal with.' No one was more condemning of the mostly Anglo-Irish landlords: 'Gross neglect of the duties inseparable from the possession of landed property is at the bottom of all this misery.'

Her best defence lies in her actions rather than her words, particularly during the famine years: in the schools she established in the teeth of clerical obstruction, the new thatch and window glass for the cabins on the estate, the toleration of rent arrears as long as there was the prospect of ways being mended, making clothing for the poor (lacking scissors, they could not make their own), the distribution of food, the denial of any luxuries for her own family, her devotion of any spare minutes to writing articles to earn money then spent on charity. In January 1847 she wrote, 'idle, improvident, reckless . . . call the bulk of the Irish what we will . . . here they are starving around us . . .' To feed them must be our business . . .'

Elizabeth Smith, while well aware of what she regarded as her proper place in Society, was equally conscious of the responsibilities accompanying it, and they were no doubt reinforced in her mind by the memory of her father's failures in this respect. She more than fulfilled them when the time came, but it is not so much for this that one reads her as for the forthright vigour, brisk wit and intelligence of her writing, the mixture of asperity with warmth of heart. And if she oversteps the mark when regularly lambasting the Irish character, it must be remembered that this was a diary, written in the heat of the moment, a healthy venting of frustrations which then allowed her to return to the task of improving their lot as best she could.

ROGER HUDSON has been braced by the Highland Lady's company ever since first encountering her in Albemarle Street in the 1970s.

Snow in the Quad

DAVID WEMYSS

I began reading C. P. Snow's 'Strangers and Brothers' series of novels in 1980. I had just started my first serious job in local government and, although I didn't know it, I was about to live through a brief golden age. The managerial future was on its way but hadn't arrived yet. I'd never even heard of a performance indicator. Still in my twenties, I emerged quickly as a bit of a legal expert (most of it bluff) and a policy adviser (most of that calculated charm). In other words, I was enjoying myself and, rather foolishly, I fancied myself as a miniature version of Lewis Eliot, Snow's largely autobiographical narrator.

I loved those books. Admittedly, there was something portentous about their sense that Eliot's endless conversations in Cambridge and Whitehall were supposed to be holding up a mirror to European history in the middle part of the twentieth century. And people certainly didn't speak like that any more, not in any circles I moved in. But of course I wished that they did.

The Masters (1951) – the fourth book in the series, and surely the quintessential tale of academic politics – was always my favourite. Rereading it during the summer (which wasn't ideal because, to begin with at least, it's definitely a *winter* novel, full of quadrangle lights

---

C. P. Snow's 'Strangers and Brothers' series comprises *George Passant* (first published as *Strangers and Brothers*, 1940), *The Light and the Dark* (1947), *Time of Hope* (1949), *The Masters* (1951), *The New Men* (1954), *Homecomings* (1956), *The Conscience of the Rich* (1958), *The Affair* (1959), *Corridors of Power* (1963), *The Sleep of Reason* (1968), and *Last Things* (1970). They are all out of print, but *The Two Cultures* (1959) is available in paperback (Cambridge University Press · 180pp · £12.99 · ISBN 9781107606142).

Mary Kuper

falling on snow and panelled walls glowing softly in firelight),
I was reminded how, in the course of all the talking, Eliot goes in for
observations about his interlocutors (and himself) that are so com-
positionally rounded that you wonder if anyone could really
accomplish such nuanced understanding in the midst of what is
often some sort of conversational miasma. First time round I had
doubts about this. But now I think it's one of Snow's finest achieve-
ments. He persuades us that these fleeting understandings *do* happen
– even if they could never be as elegant as his portrayals of them.

I said it was a winter novel. Here's what I mean:

The snow had only just stopped, and in the court below my
rooms all sounds were dulled. There were few sounds to hear,
for it was early in January, and the college was empty and quiet;
I could just make out the footsteps of the porter, as he passed
beneath the window on his last round of the night. Now and
again his keys clinked, and the clink reached me after the pad
of his footsteps had been lost in the snow. I had drawn my cur-

tains early that evening and not moved out. The kitchens had sent up a meal, and I had eaten it as I read by the fire.

The Master of an unnamed Cambridge college is dying, and a new Master will have to be elected. The stylish tiptoeing begins at once.

'In a few weeks, in a few months at most, the college will have to elect a new Master.'
    'Yes,' I said.
    'When the time arrives, we shall have to do it in a hurry,' said Jago. 'I suppose before then we shall have made up our minds whom we are going to elect.'
    I had known, for minutes past, that this was coming. I had not wanted to talk of it that night. Jago was longing for me to say that he ought to be the next Master, that my own mind was made up, that I should vote for him. He had longed for me to say it without prompting; he had not wanted even to mention the election. It was anguish for him to make the faintest hint without response. Yet he was impelled to go on, he could not stop. It harassed me to see this proud man humiliating himself.

'It was anguish for him to make the faintest hint without response.' That's what I mean about nuanced understanding in the midst of conversational miasma. Eliot sees that his interlocutor wants to be the author of felicitous remarks *and* the author of their reception. It's like fishing for compliments, but it veers between spontaneity and manipulation. All in all, quite a deep observation.
    However, Snow isn't supposed to be deep; in fact he's often called mediocre and formulaic, and all that stuff about footsteps in quadrangle snow and panelled walls bathed in firelight does sometimes look as if it's been put there almost lazily, to elicit the most predictable of responses. Yet most of the time he gets away with it – even if you do occasionally feel that you're enjoying literary comfort food.

But no one ever said that this was going to be a modernist stream-of-consciousness evocation. It's a middlebrow yarn, full of dialogue, not exactly fast-moving but strangely gripping. And there's something deceptively memorable about those predictable responses. People say you're not happy if you're noticing it, but then again there are moments when you feel you're definitely alive, and those you *do* notice. Or the memory of such a moment can make you wonder if you'll ever feel that alive again. The muffled sounds of Snow's wintry colleges, the sheets of rain blowing across his Whitehall streetscapes, do somehow catch the pathos of noticing. And, in the end, what's so bad about comfort food? He may be cheating a bit – and we're not working very hard – but we're moved anyway.

Any ambivalence disappears when you get into the real momentum of the story, which I suppose you have to characterize in terms of psychological observation. The election is going to be close, and two rival camps quickly emerge. Then misgivings and doubts begin to set in. These are subtly shaded and wordy, but the story is never heavy going. The setting is rarefied, but the fluctuations of the human heart remain the same.

Nowadays, though, Snow is probably best remembered not for his novels but for the lecture 'The Two Cultures and the Scientific Revolution' which he delivered at Cambridge in 1959. A physicist and chemist as well as a civil servant and novelist, he argued that intellectual life in Western society was damagingly split between scientists and literary types, and that the latter were more culpable. Some scientists couldn't cope with Dickens, which was nothing to be proud of, but others had embraced literature. Humanities scholars, on the other hand, were unlikely to have even the remotest idea about the second law of thermodynamics, and didn't see why they should.

Warming to his theme, Snow even claimed that scientists had 'the future in their bones', whereas 'the traditional culture responded by wishing the future did not exist'. He also emphasized the importance of scientifically literate politicians, and the danger of overly literary ones. A lifelong socialist, he was suspicious of fascist tendencies in the likes of Yeats and Ezra Pound, although, in his lecture, he attributed the suspicion to 'a scientist of distinction' as a smokescreen for airing the idea that Yeats and Pound bore some sort of responsibility for Auschwitz.

Otherwise he was unequivocal. Science was the only viable solution to narrowing the catastrophic gaps in wealth that were emerging all over the world. If the democracies didn't modernize undeveloped countries, Snow argued, the Communist countries would do it instead – leaving the West stranded as an enclave in a different world. Only by asserting science (over and against the quietism or élitism of literary inclinations) could disaster be averted. But, at their best, the humanities still exuded a unique hospitality of spirit – although that now sounds a bit outmoded.

In a way, the lecture was a symptom of the Cold War. It claimed that technologically progressive (but humane) socialism was the only way to seize the moral high ground from totalitarian Marxism. To that extent, it was off the mark. I suppose you have to say that capitalism won the moral and economic arguments. But, then again, many think that Marxism sneaked the cultural one without anyone noticing. Nowadays, many humanities scholars know their thermodynamics but think the Western literary canon is out-of-date and élitist. I don't think Snow saw that one coming.

Anyway, whatever you think of them, these themes are also the themes of the 'Strangers and Brothers' series. In *The Masters*, the rivalry is between a traditionalist and a politically progressive scientist. Lewis Eliot is a man of the Left, but he will not let that blind him to the greater human breadth of the more reactionary of the two candidates. *The New Men* (1954) is about the emergence of the atomic bomb. *Corridors of Power* (1963) sees Eliot helping a Conservative MP who is disquieted by this threat. *The Affair* (1959) isn't about a love affair but scientific fraud, and the ethical atmosphere of the tale is another reminder that Snow was never just crudely pro-science. Scientific fraud is seen as a terrible breach of faith in a very old-fashioned way.

And this is strangely apposite to the public policy conundrums of our own time. Today, our politicians have become more scientifically literate as they wrestle with things like climate change, but the public has become suspicious of politicized science – something else Snow didn't see coming.

And he took for granted something we now find very noticeable. As I've already hinted, one of the distinctive things about the 'Strangers and Brothers' books is how the characters regularly extemporize and surprise themselves in everyday talk. It's an arresting quality because you rarely encounter it any more. But isn't it what the humanities at their best can bring to scientific culture, and to public policy across the board? Perhaps those outmoded ideals of shared enjoyment in conversation – ideals that no doubt seemed to be of diminishing importance in 1959 – might yet make a comeback.

Maybe that's wishful thinking. And, one way or another, it won't turn Snow into a great novelist. But, as readers of *Slightly Foxed* know, there are a lot of readable and lovable novels out there that are never going to be called great but which still punch above their weight. Snow, I think, is in this category. His storytelling doesn't succeed in spite of his political agenda; it succeeds because the agenda is so fluid and understated.

DAVID WEMYSS graduated in law from the University of Aberdeen in 1977 and worked in local government in that city until he retired in 2011. He continues to live there with his wife and son.

The Mouse that Roared

BELINDA HOLLYER

When I was 9 and at primary school in New Zealand, my class teacher was a poet called Kendrick Smithyman. He was a rather bad-tempered curmudgeon but he had an overwhelming advantage over any other teacher I'd met: he read lots of good poetry to us, and the books he chose for class serialization were brilliant. I remember many of the poems he introduced us to, but most of all I still treasure the first book he read to us. It was E. B. White's *Stuart Little*.

Most young readers these days have probably encountered White's *Charlotte's Web*, a later and an almost-perfect book as well as a tear-jerker of major proportions, with one of the very best opening lines in modern literature – '"Where's Papa going with that axe?" said Fern to her mother as they were setting the table for breakfast.' When I was 9 I'd never heard of the author or his books, but I fell in love with *Stuart Little*, the book and protagonist both, and I've never really recovered.

E. B. (Elwyn Brooks, but known as Andy) White was a highly respected staff writer for *The New Yorker* and columnist for *Harper's* magazine. (In later years he also produced a revised version of *The Elements of Style*, the classic American style guide, now commonly known as Strunk & White.) He wrote exclusively and seriously for adults: no one could have expected a children's novel from him. But it seems that privately he'd long cherished the idea of writing a children's story about a mouse: he had nephews and nieces who begged stories from him, and he'd dreamed of a small character with the features of

The Puffin edition of E. B. White's *Stuart Little* (1945) contains Garth Williams's original illustrations: Pb · 144pp · £5.99 · ISBN 9780141305066.

a mouse: 'nicely dressed, courageous and questing'. He stocked a desk drawer with fragments about his mouse-child, named Stuart.

White sent an unfinished version of the book to his editor at Harper & Brothers in 1939, but the final version wasn't submitted until 1945, when he delivered it to the great Ursula Nordstrom, then the director of Harper's Department of Books for Boys and Girls. *Stuart Little* was published in October of that year, with illustrations by Garth Williams and an initial printing of 50,000 copies.

The book begins:

> When Mrs Frederick C. Little's second son was born, everyone noticed that he was not much bigger than a mouse. The truth of the matter was, the baby looked very much like a mouse in every way. He was only about two inches high; and he had a mouse's sharp nose, a mouse's whiskers, and the pleasant, shy manner of a mouse. Before he was many days old he was not only looking like a mouse but acting like one too – wearing a grey hat and carrying a small cane. Mr and Mrs Little named him Stuart, and Mr Little made him a tiny bed out of four clothespins and a cigarette box.

In the way of young readers I saw no problem with any of that: it was an unusual but perfectly acceptable start to a story, and the suspension of disbelief was easily made. Stuart is a quirky character, full of an appealing

Garth Williams

practical energy. He is helpful around the house, retrieving Mrs Little's lost ring from the drain – his human brother George lowers him down the bathroom plughole on a string – and he finds imaginative ways to survive in the outside world. Stuart has satisfyingly dangerous adventures – sailing a toy boat on the Central Park lake; being trapped on a garbage scow and towed out to sea; and having several hazardous encounters with the Littles' cat, Snowball.

The story is also, and often, very funny. Mr and Mrs Little edit the rhymes in children's books to correct the way mice are portrayed, and Mr Little encourages his wife to tear the 'Three Blind Mice' page from the nursery songbook. "'I don't want Stuart to get a lot of notions in his head," said Mr Little. "I should feel badly to have my son growing up fearing that a farmer's wife was going to cut off his tail with a carving knife."' They worry about the demeaning characterization of mice in the poem which begins: ''Twas the night before Christmas when all through the house / Not a creature was stirring, not even a mouse.' "'I think it might embarrass Stuart to hear mice mentioned in such a belittling manner," said Mrs Little, and she carefully substituted the word "louse" for mouse in the book.'

There's also a delightful chapter in which Stuart takes a class of children when their regular teacher is ill, and guides them into suggesting good laws for the world. 'Nix on swiping anything' is accepted, and so is 'absolutely no being mean'. Stuart then prompts the class to act out these laws, with very satisfying results.

But despite its humour and energy, the book ends with uncertainty rather than resolution. Stuart falls in love with a bird called Margalo, and when she flies away he leaves home to look for her. With the courage of a questing hero he 'started up the road that led to the north . . . As he peered into the great land that stretched before him, the way seemed long. But the sky was bright, and he somehow felt he was headed in the right direction.' Stuart was the first romantic hero I encountered in a book: a worthy and complex one.

The critical response to the publication of *Stuart Little* was surprisingly mixed. Anne Carroll Moore, the fearsomely influential and powerful children's librarian at the New York Public Library, was, quite frankly, horrified. She had learned of the possibility of a children's book written by E. B. White; she had written to him several times to entice him into her grasp; she had waited in her majestic fashion for his book to be finished. 'No one will be more interested than I when your children's book is ready,' she wrote to him. She was eager to take credit for it, but the book she finally read in galley proofs . . . well!

That was quite another matter. 'I was never so disappointed by a book in my life,' she declared. She told Ursula Nordstrom that the book 'mustn't be published'. And she struck a blow to support that assertion, saying threateningly that the book 'will be very difficult to place in libraries and schools over the country'.

Miss Moore had retired by 1945 but her influence was still pervasive, and her successor at the New York Public Library refused, when prompted, to buy *Stuart Little*. 'Not recommended for purchase by expert' was the message conveyed to libraries across America – Miss Moore had left her special refusal stamp on her desk for future use. (It later emerged that her browbeaten successor had bought a copy, but she kept it under her desk until the library's director heard of the book, read and loved it, and ordered Stuart out of his hiding-place.)

Ursula Nordstrom later remembered that watching Anne Carroll Moore's attempt to block the publication of *Stuart Little* was like watching a horse fall down, 'its spindly legs crumbling beneath its great weight'. She was not, however, the only objector – Harold Ross, the founding editor of *The New Yorker*, stuck his head into White's office one afternoon and said: 'God damn it, White, at least you could have had him adopted.' Even Edmund Wilson intervened, telling White that he should have developed the theme 'more in the manner of Kafka'. But the author and the book's young readers remained relatively unruffled, and the book sold 100,000 copies within fifteen months of publication.

I still have my original hardback of *Stuart Little*, begged from my parents as a birthday present after I'd listened to the book in class. It's the Hamish Hamilton edition, first published in 1946 and reprinted in 1955. Its dust-jacket fell apart years ago but at some stage I carefully stuck the front-cover illustration inside: Garth Williams's picture of Stuart in his shorts and shirtsleeves paddling a tiny birch bark canoe called 'Summer Memories'. The cover is printed in only three colours and yet the illustration's charm shines through. One modern paperback cover now features a picture from inside the book, fully coloured for the occasion: Stuart swinging a tiny wooden hammer so that he can use the bathroom tap. It's lively and amusing, but it lacks the plangent wistfulness of the canoe scene. (Garth Williams, according to Eugene Exman's 1967 publishing history of Harper, made the ninth submission of possible artwork, which was the first to meet with Nordstrom and White's approval. Jill Lepore, in an article in *The New Yorker* in 2008, put the count at eight. Either way, his work was well worth waiting for.)

Garth Williams

I love *Charlotte's Web*, and I regularly read it to 8- and 9-year-olds when I was a teacher. (All teachers and parents who attempt this task will know to brace themselves for the inevitable tears when Charlotte dies alone. I think it's the 'alone' that does it.) But *Stuart Little* remains my favourite children's novel, perhaps because of its imperfections. You could say that the ending is too abrupt, or too full of doubt for a children's book. You could say that the arc of story isn't properly realized. You could say that *Charlotte's Web* is a better children's book. And you might be right about all that, but *Stuart Little* is more than a children's book: it transcends such an artificial label. Its themes are universal ones, and its unresolved ending is a true stroke of genius. Stuart is indeed headed in the right direction at the end of the book – into the complexities, pleasures and pains of real life. I got a sense of all that when I was 9, and it's shaped my reading pleasures ever since.

BELINDA HOLLYER has spent most of her working life enjoying some combination of children and books. She is presently tussling with revisions to her fifth novel for young readers, and wondering if adding a mouse might help . . .

Inside the Inside Man

MATT HUBER

The spines are fading now and advancing higher up the shelves in second-hand bookshops. Yet, when glimpsed, the word 'Inside' in their titles tells all – these are the journalistic documentary works of John Gunther.

Inside Europe, Inside USA, Inside Russia . . . if journalism is the first draft of history, John Gunther's journalistic documentary works are indisputably dated – his last, *Inside Australia*, had to be co-authored and was published in 1972, two years after his death. The books are time-capsules: all the world leaders and political figures featured in the *Inside* series – and they focus primarily on leaders and politicians – are long gone. Gunther's style, however, is still most vividly alive. He was first and foremost a reporter, and throughout his books an immediate journalistic active-case style dominates – short, punchy sentences such as 'Hitler rants. He orates. He seldom answers questions.' And: 'If Stalin has nerves, they are veins in rock.'

These quotations are from his first book, *Inside Europe*, first published in 1936 and updated in no less than twenty-six editions over two years – quite a publishing feat in the turbulent pre-war period. In his own memoir about his writing entitled *Inside the Inside Books* (1962), Gunther tells how, as an already-busy European newspaper correspondent, he did all he could to evade taking on what was to

John Gunther, *Inside Europe* (1936), *Inside Asia* (1939), *Inside Latin America* (1941), *Inside USA* (1947), *Behind Europe's Curtain* (1949), *Death Be Not Proud* (1949), *Inside Africa* (1955), *Inside Russia Today* (1958) and *The Lost City* (1964) are out of print as is Ken Cuthbertson's *Inside: The Biography of John Gunther* (1992).

become *Inside Europe*. In 1934 his publisher, Cass Canfield of Harper & Brothers, had to track Gunther down to a hotel in Vienna and sit on his bed to get him to agree to the project. On its publication, the book not only sold well but also won praise. The diplomat and diarist Harold Nicolson called *Inside Europe* 'a serious contribution to contemporary knowledge. This is one of the most educative as well as one of the most exciting books I have read for years.'

What of John Gunther the man? To me he seems to typify, possibly unfairly, the tough American newspaper reporter of the pre-war period. Born in Chicago in 1901, and therefore growing up with the century whose events he was to chronicle, he joined the *Chicago Daily News* as a reporter at the age of 21. In 1934 he was in Europe as the newspaper's bureau chief in London, working successively in Berlin, Vienna, Moscow, Rome and Paris, in what he called the 'bubbling, blazing days of American foreign correspondence in Europe . . . before journalism became institutionalized. We were scavengers, buzzards, out to get the news no matter whose wings got clipped.'

In those days of emerging dictatorships, local wars and only rudimentary air travel, he managed to hop around Europe interviewing everyone who mattered. His primary focus was always on leadership, on power – summed up in his own question, 'Who runs this place?' He believed that 'the accidents of personality play a great role in history'.

In his memoir Gunther lists questions that he always tried to put to political leaders; one he cites as 'What are his fundamental sources of power?' (There are very few 'hers' in the *Inside* series.) Knowing this, the reader can see the structures of support behind and beneath leaders from Hitler, Mussolini and Stalin to De Valera, Piłsudski and Churchill – and the benefits for the author of a chilly car ride through the Ebbw Vale coalfields with Aneurin Bevan. His chapter on the Romania of the colourful King Carol and his court could be pure Broadway musical comedy were it not for that country's corruption. Reading the yellowing and invariably foxed books now, one cannot help but wear the spectacles of hindsight; yet Gunther was frequently spot-on in his predictions – including the certainty of war as a result of the rise of Hitler, and the eventual emergence of Churchill, then in his 'wilderness' period. 'Millions', he wrote in 1936, 'depend for life or death on the will of Hitler, Mussolini, Stalin. Never have politics been so vital and dynamic as today.'

The phrase aptly describes Gunther's writing style – nothing dry or overly academic there; one of his sub-heads is simply: 'More Fascist scurvy'. Both his full profiles and his shorter 'pocket' summaries of political, military, business and social figures are vibrant with colour; one British lady, he said, credited him with 'treating gossip in the grand manner'.

And he didn't stop at Europe. At the end of the Thirties, along with his wife Frances, he visited eighteen Asian countries in ten months for the volume that would be published in 1939 as *Inside Asia*. His travels included overflying the Khyber Pass standing in the open cockpit of a fighter plane. And onwards: after revising *Inside Europe* yet again he set about tackling Latin America, travelling over 18,000 miles by air from Mexico to the Straits of Magellan, and interviewing on average twenty leading people per country, a total of over 400 interviews. Like its predecessors, the work contains nuggets of Gunther colour. Of the Argentinian leader General Justo he observed: 'He likes to eat chocolates rapidly one after another.' That the book did not contain a single mention of Juan and Evita Perón, who were to dominate Argentina's politics a decade later, only demonstrates the transient nature of both politics and journalism.

After reporting the Second World War in the Mediterranean and Europe, Gunther went home, so to speak, to research and write *Inside USA*. By this time, he said, he 'cared less what a dictator ate for breakfast'. Yet his state-by-state analysis is full of colourful detail, from the hyperactive Mayor of New York, Fiorello La Guardia, to the shenanigans of Governor Huey Long in Louisiana. Pointing up the transience of Gunther's books are the single-line mentions of future presidents such as John F. Kennedy – 'an attractive youngster';

Richard Nixon – 'a noisy congressman'; and Lyndon Johnson – 'well-liked by the middle citizenry . . . of Texas'.

Inside USA was poignant in its timing. Gunther said the book had been the suggestion of his son and only surviving child, Johnny, and it is to the youngster, only 17 when he died of a brain tumour in 1947, that the book is dedicated. One's vision of a hard-boiled newspaperman ready to ride roughshod over his subjects' feelings in his deadline-driven rush to judgement is shaken by Gunther's handling of his son's fate. After *Inside USA*, Gunther and Frances wrote the ineffably moving narrative, *Death Be Not Proud* (from John Donne), the story of his son's life, his illness and his parents' vain quest for successful treatment.

John Gunther the journalist-writer managed to go on, travelling again in post-war Europe's newly Communist countries. Reading *Behind Europe's Curtain* today one can see the broken people, the dank rubble, the makeshift street furniture, and smell the boiled dumplings and potatoes of broken and battered cities like Berlin and Warsaw. In the mid-Fifties he produced yet another continental doorstopper, *Inside Africa*. Here, conducting 1,500 interviews and still master of the colourful nugget, he described one African *Scoop*-like state where dignitaries wore top hats to social occasions in order to facilitate thieving, the budget for brass bands exceeded that for public health and an official communiqué reported: 'Tommy guns announced the arrival of the guests of honour.'

He wrote lengthy profiles – of Eisenhower, MacArthur, Roosevelt – and followed *Inside Africa* with *Inside Russia* three years later. He produced novels too, including *The Lost City*, reflecting his time in pre-war Vienna.

I first picked up *Inside Europe* as a teenager in a second-hand bookshop in Dorking. Having been brought up on dry history at school, I was enchanted by a pre-war Europe I hadn't of course experienced, as well as the journalistic style I still admire fifty years on. Tips for budding journalists abound; as a reporter who only took written notes – never a tape recorder – Gunther reveals how he often got his most revelatory quotes once he'd slipped his notebook into his pocket, at which point his subjects felt they could relax.

When a couple of years later Anthony Sampson produced his first *Anatomy of Britain* in 1962, one could see shades of Gunther in Sampson's own seeking out of the sources of British power. Sampson acknowledged this with the final book in the *Anatomy* series, published in 2004 and titled *Who Runs This Place?*

Gunther can be credited with founding modern-day 'book journalism'. Incredibly he had no team of researchers and seems to have travelled only with his wives, first Frances and then Jane. But what do his *Inside* books and his prolific output generally offer to the bibliophile of today? He wrote primarily for an American readership so his books have recurring touches of provincialism. But anyone wanting to see how Europe's terrible fate was already evident in the mid-Thirties should find and read *Inside Europe*. And there's more: whether he's in Paraguay, Thailand or Australia, or inside General Eisenhower's office at SHAPE, over half a century later his writing remains vital and fresh. In three highly productive decades, he interviewed most world leaders and wrote profiles of political leadership in practically every country of the world – producing books that could well serve as set texts for the lesson of history.

John Gunther was published in Britain by Hamish Hamilton, to whom he paid tribute, along with Cass Canfield, for getting the *Inside* books going. He died in New York in 1970, aged 69. If you can find them, his books pretty much contain his life, though a biography by Ken Cuthbertson was published in 1992.

MATT HUBER started working life as a newspaper journalist and wishes he'd had the nerve to stick with it. Now he studies history, writes unpublished fiction – and worries about Putin's Russia.

An Elevated Lifestyle

GUS ALEXANDER

The amazing thing about Nero Wolfe, hero of Rex Stout's *Fer-de-Lance*, was that he lived in a house with its own elevator. I was 14 when I first read the book. I was spending the school holidays with my mother and brand-new stepfather, who were then living on an oil pumping station in Iraq with the evocative Babylonian name of K3. The British expatriate staff lived in prefabricated bungalows assembled in various configurations to give the illusion of variety. These were commodious, well-planned and, when the air conditioning worked, comfortable, but characterless. And here was a private detective who lived in an enormous townhouse with its own passenger lift.

Not only that, it had a separate goods elevator to a special orchid-growing house on the roof, and any number of intercoms, alarms, built-in recording devices and electric safes. It even had a gourmet kitchen with its own entrance. Right on Wolfe's doorstep were a dozen drugstores, delis, dry-cleaners and scores of cinemas. On K3 there was a single weekly showing of an ancient black-and-white film in the outdoor cinema, where, like Eric Morecambe, they played all the right reels but not necessarily in the right order.

Fer-de-Lance is the first in a series of

Gus Alexander

Rex Stout, *Fer-de-Lance* (1934), is out of print.

48 detective novels (or mystery stories as their author styled them). Starting in 1934, when he was 48, Stout spun out an average of one a year until his death in 1975. His hero, Nero Wolfe, is an enormously corpulent man who charges vast sums of money to people who need to hire New York's finest private investigator – although Wolfe is keen to stress that he is essentially an intuitive artist, not merely a consulting detective. Apart from being huge, or perhaps as a result of being huge, Wolfe likes to move as little as possible, and by the time we are introduced to him he has established a routine that enables him to live an agreeable life more or less without having to move at all. Obviously he needs to earn a living, which means taking on cases, which generally means movement, but unless his coffers are virtually empty, he is mostly reluctant to do even that.

Wolfe is modelled on the cerebral English detective, and thus has a great brain that needs to be nourished. Unlike his American contemporaries Sam Spade, Lew Harper and Philip Marlowe, Wolfe does not need to solve mysteries by sticking guns in people's faces, or driving dames around in his convertible, or sorting out uncooperative witnesses with fisticuffs. Wolfe's brain is nourished by his love of breeding orchids, which he does between 9 and 11 every morning, and between 4 and 6 every afternoon. We English outcasts in K3 would have killed to cultivate a square foot of lawn. Wolfe's elevator lifts him to the plant rooms on the roof, the domain of Theo Horstmann, one of the three people with whom he shares his vast brownstone house on New York's West 35th Street.

Theo is Wolfe's gardener/horticulturist/botanist, the begetter and keeper of the sacred *Orchidaceae* who helps Wolfe to tend, breed, propagate and even hybridize the exotic flora. Horstmann keeps track of other breeders and is constantly on the lookout for seedlings and rare imports. Occasionally, very occasionally, clients are treated to a tour of this private display, and in very rare instances are even made a present of a bloom. It is not absolutely forbidden for Wolfe to be disturbed while cloistered with his plants, but there is no emergency under the sun that will allow him to be called away during the allocated orchid-tending hours.

Wolfe's considerable frame is nourished by Fritz Brenner, his chef and butler, whose culinary reputation ensures that would-be interrogatees can be persuaded to travel great distances when offered the opportunity to sample Wolfe's table. Fritz manages the kitchen at the bottom of the house and provides an endless supply of gourmet breakfasts, elevenses, lunches, teas, dinners, picnics and late-night snacks. He also looks after Wolfe's supply of beer. At the beginning of *Fer-de-Lance*, we discover that Wolfe is cutting down to 10 quarts a day. Thus, quite a large proportion of his waking life is spent taking the tops off, checking the temperature of, pouring the contents from, and discarding the empty bottles that accrue to this ritual, not to mention actually drinking the stuff. It never occurred to me that gaseous American beer might be considered an unusual complement to, say, a Tabasco crayfish and asparagus soufflé. At 14 I was allowed a small glass of beer as a special treat, and here was this chap virtually living on it.

Everything else in Wolfe's life – cars, guns, gumshoe work, snappy dialogue, schmoozing and billing clients, interviewing people and persuading them to visit Wolfe in his brownstone, where they will be relentlessly cross-examined – is dealt with by Wolfe's wiseacre sidekick, Archie Goodwin. Goodwin is Wolfe's amanuensis. It is he who writes up the cases, and it is from his viewpoint that the stories are told. Goodwin is 32, fit, a snappy dresser and an orphan. At the time of this story he has been working for Wolfe for five years, although he realizes, as does Wolfe, that one day he will have to leave, grow up and settle down. Archie knows news reporters, beat cops, collection agents and ex-DAs, and can be relied upon to charm female secretaries into divulging information they might more prudently have kept to themselves.

Nero Wolfe mysteries provide a distraction at Totleigh Towers, so it should have been no surprise to discover that P. G. Wodehouse and

Stout were friends and admirers of one another's work. The reader enjoys both writers for the same reasons – the familiar cast of characters, the milieu, the period detail, the relentless storytelling and, above all, the style. Wodehouse said that he'd read Stout's stories many times and so knew what happened, but they continued to give him pleasure because of the way they were told.

Like Bertie Wooster writing of Jeeves, Goodwin is in awe of Wolfe's great brain. Although he is bright and intuitive himself, and knows how the world works, he can never outguess his employer. '"You know it for a fact when you are presented with it, Archie, but you have no feeling for phenomena." After I'd looked up the word phenomena in the dictionary I couldn't see that he had anything, but there was no use arguing with him.'

Wholly unlike Wooster, Goodwin is capable, diligent, sassy and all-American. A good man to have with you in a tight spot, and effortlessly (and rather irritatingly) successful with women. Goodwin does the driving, but unlike Wooster, Wolfe virtually never accompanies him, although he supplies an enormous black roadster which he insists is kept in immaculate condition at all times, in case a client needs to be collected. This spends its nights coddled in a garage two blocks away, quite a hike in New York City. In slack periods, collecting and delivering the roadster seems to be the only exercise that Goodwin ever gets.

From 1906 to 1908 Stout served in the US Navy, where he was quartered aboard Teddy Roosevelt's presidential yacht. This would have been years ahead of the White House in terms of the advanced 'residential' technology it enjoyed, and the pneumatics, intercoms, air conditioning, communications, food refrigeration and built-in furniture all find their way into the fabric of Wolfe's brownstone.

Early in his career Stout had invented a banking system that enabled schools to manage the individual savings accounts that they encouraged their pupils to open. The system was adopted by several hundred schools across the country, and Stout was paid a royalty.

This enabled him to travel around Europe, where he wrote several novels and learned everything about everything, particularly about what was good to eat and the way to tell someone how to make it for him. He lost everything in the stock-market crash of 1929 and so had to return to America and begin writing in earnest. *Fer-de-Lance*, and with it the Nero Wolfe ensemble, appeared four years later.

Wolfe's pampered and agreeable lifestyle is not cheap, of course. One has no idea about Sherlock Holmes's finances beyond knowing that he slips his Baker Street irregulars a sixpence from time to time, but Wolfe demonstrates an instinctive understanding of just how much clients need him, and thus how much they can be persuaded to pay. His charges are carefully spelt out in terms of his own fee, his expenses, his retainers, disbursements, special appointments and bonuses. Wolfe is reluctant to take on the case introduced in *Fer-de-Lance*, intriguing as it appears, because he cannot identify an obvious invoicee. He becomes more enthusiastic once he hears that the murder victim's millionaire widow, unhappy that the police have failed to discover her husband's murderer, has offered a prize of $50,000 to whoever will do so. That's $3 million by today's reckoning, so would pay for a lot of time with orchids.

Although *Fer-de-Lance* ('after the Bushmaster, Archie, the second most poisonous of all the South American vipers') is the first of the Nero Wolfe mysteries, Archie Goodwin recounts the case as though his reader has been following his tales of Wolfe's brilliance for years, and the routine at West 35th Street is described on the assumption that it is wholly familiar. The layout of the house, the strict office hours, the lifts, the routine with the plants, Wolfe's custom-built chair, the red chair that the clients sit in, the arrangement with the front-door buzzer, the fitted carpets everywhere (very unusual in 1934) are all referred to as though we've practically stayed there.

Although the novels appeared over a period of thirty years they are effectively contemporary. Goodwin presumes familiarity with earlier adventures and with Wolfe's other hirelings – Saul Panzer, Fred

Durkin and Orrie Cather, who carry out Wolfe's pavement work and provide muscle. Only his nemesis, Inspector L. T. Cramer, doesn't appear in *Fer-de-Lance*, although his office is referred to. The fact that Wolfe runs rings round the police is a constant theme, as is his habit of only divulging scraps of information on a 'need-to-know basis'. Wolfe is a great aphorist: 'Any spoke will lead an ant to the hub' or 'No Archie,' he says when it is suggested that he borrow money during a temporary income drought, 'Nature has arranged that when you overcome a given inertia the resulting momentum is proportionate. If I were to begin borrowing money, I would end up by devising means to persuade the Secretary of State to lend me the Gold Reserve.' Wolfe's universal expression of contempt is 'Pfui'.

The cases present themselves. Wolfe sifts the evidence and sends Archie hither and thither to interview suspects and look for holes in incomplete narratives. Once Archie has reported back and the mystery begins to unfold, Wolfe calls for the various parties to be questioned and/or summoned.

As the evidence accumulates, Wolfe takes stock. In silence Goodwin watches him exercising his formidable brain, sitting behind his desk in his specially engineered chair, eyes closed, fingers interlaced over his chest, lips pursing in and out as he concentrates his marvellous brain on the problem, Goodwin waiting by the telephone for instructions to summon all parties to the dénouement.

As a formula it never fails to engage, and the *mise-en-scène* continues to delight, even though Wolfe's culinary delights can now be seen in every weekend supplement, and *Cattleya laelia*, wrapped in cellophane, can be had from London's Columbia Road flower market at fifteen quid for two.

GUS ALEXANDER runs an architect's practice in Smithfield. He has squeezed lifts into a hotel or two, and a few hostels, but he's still waiting to be asked to fit one into a private house.

All in the Mind?

SARAH CROWDEN

I have long wanted to offer an update on the latest additions to the Crowden Archive. Some subscribers may recall the first piece on the subject, 'Something for the Weekend' in *Slightly Foxed* No. 32. In it, I described a selection of the titles in my possession which have been collected over more than thirty years and which appeal to those possessed of a Lower Fourth Form sense of humour. My mother feels that I should now move on to more suitable pastimes, pokerwork, perhaps, or tatting, but books with questionable titles just keep on falling into my hands.

My intention has always been to leave the archive to my various scouts who have, over the years, been kind enough to contribute to it. Benjamin Whitrow, a fellow-actor, is a new recruit to the band of overgrown schoolboys who scour bookshops on my behalf in London and the provinces. Last Christmas he produced *Smiling Willie and the Tiger* and *I'll Come if You Will*. I have bookended the latter with *Taken by the Hand* and *Sooty's Jumbo Trouble*. Ben's scouting skills are sorely needed, because my Yorkshire scout no longer passes on duplicate finds and my solicitor, an early recruit, has promised *Biggles Takes It Rough* but has yet to deliver.

All archive books have to be bought cheap, as I am still of the opinion that no title should cost more than £5, and I'm afraid I think purchasing over the Internet is cheating. *Pansie's Flour Bin*, an obscure nineteenth-century title, failed on both counts, which was a great disappointment.

Inspired by a visit to the *Slightly Foxed* office, two doors up from a saucy emporium for ladies and a short bus ride from 100 Shades of

Blue, which is not a paint shop specializing in Farrow and Ball emulsion, I returned home to tackle the books, now four deep on each shelf. A Dewey system unique to the archive has had to be created: Dicks now fill more than half a shelf, Queens the other half. Underneath those are a baker's dozen Enid Blytons, including *Mr Pink Whistle Interferes*.

My husband, a gardener, is particularly fond of *Do It Yourself in the Garden*, published in the 1950s, which is under a new category, 'Household'. I began this one when offered a copy of *Christie's Old Organ* by a subscriber, next to which I intended to put *Archie's Old Desk*. Alas, the former never arrived, and is probably languishing in HM Customs. 'Household' now includes *Rational Cookery* (is there irrational cookery?), *The Radiation Cookbook* and *The Right Way to Keep Cats* (there's a wrong way?) by Kit Wilson, who, as it turns out, was a well-known cat-show judge. I intend to add *Confessions of a Decanter* and *The Empty Jam Pot* if they ever turn up.

'Euphemisms' includes *Star Probe*, *Trader Horn*, *Every Common Bush*, *Young Man with a Horn* and *Little Boy Blue's Horn* (a children's book). Under 'Toilet Humour', Nevil Shute has crept in with *Round the Bend*, which I have placed hard by *Constipation and Our Civilization*, *Tom Cringle's Log* and *Period Stuff* by Dornford Yates. I just wish I could add to these a title discovered in the index of another book: *Hope for Number Two, Help from Number One*. It's quite rare, but perhaps a subscriber might oblige.

Dust-jackets continue to be a source of deep joy. Who could not love the drawing on the front of *Stormcock Meets Trouble* which seems so innocuous at first, until a closer look reveals that the illustrator must have had a grudge against the publisher. One artist in particular I simply cannot trace, despite extensive research. His illustrations for two 1950s books, the infamous *Queer Doings at Quantham* and *Ready, Aye Ready*, suggest something else entirely is going on between the covers.

There's no new sheet music in the archive at present, though I have been promised a couple of corkers, but while they take their time to arrive, play titles are a new source of levity: *Four Queens Wait for Henry* has not been performed for years, though my researches show that *Stop It, Nurse* is a popular choice for amateur dramatic societies in Ireland. *I Killed the Count* (a James Naughtie moment if ever there was one), *Sit down a Minute, Adrian* and *Hot and Cold in All Rooms* are no longer in the repertoire of the Royal Shakespeare Company or the National Theatre, and since repertory theatre is more or less defunct, they are unlikely to be put on again. Despite the high ticket prices in London's West End, I personally would book two seats in the front stalls to see a production of *Radiance: The Passion of Marie Curie*, having missed *Married Love*, a play based on the life of contraceptive pioneer Marie Stopes, which ran at Wyndham's Theatre in 1988 for a matter of weeks.

Some of my titles resonate more than others: *Birds I Have Known* reminds me of 1960s sitcoms. *Darcy, The Young Acrobat* evokes the most delicious visions of Colin Firth in a mankini. *Simplified Dog Cures* will be the first loan from the archive to Chudleigh, resident office dog at *Slightly Foxed*.

I still search, fruitlessly thus far, for *Roger the Missionary* and *Weymouth: The English Naples*, and now wish to add a further request to subscribers: if anyone has a spare copy of *A Man, Every Inch of Him* or *Peter Darington, Seaman Detective*, please send them to me via the *Slightly Foxed* office. Postage will of course be reimbursed.

In the meantime, the last word must rest with my beloved Romanian phrasebook published in 1936. *English Words for All Occasions* contains much useful advice. A sub-heading, 'Intellect', under the main heading 'Education', offers the exhortation 'Don't mutter when you're reading', which, with regard to this article, would be entirely appropriate for those who read *Slightly Foxed* on public transport.

SARAH CROWDEN has a Foundation Certificate in Bricklaying. Suggestive terminology in bricklaying is limited, but she is delighted to report that it is rife in Plumbing.

Bibliography

John Betjeman, *Collected Poems*   54

Christopher Booker, *The Seven Basic Plots: Why We Tell Stories*   43

Angela Brazil, *The Manor House School; The School by the Sea; For the Sake of the School; The Luckiest Girl in the School; For the School Colours; A Patriotic Schoolgirl*   26

John Buchan, *Mr Standfast*   7

Truman Capote, *Breakfast at Tiffany's*   60

Gerald Durrell, *My Family and Other Animals*   14

The Encyclopaedia Britannica   20

E. M. Forster, *Two Cheers for Democracy*   33

Elizabeth Grant, *Memoirs of a Highland Lady*   65

John Gunther, *Inside Europe* and his other *Inside* books   81

L. P. Hartley, *The Shrimp and the Anemone; The Sixth Heaven; Eustace and Hilda*   38

Patrick O'Brian, *Master and Commander; Post Captain; HMS Surprise; The Mauritius Command; Desolation Island; The Fortune of War; The Surgeon's Mate; The Ionian Mission; Treason's Harbour; The Far Side of the World; The Reverse of the Medal; The Letter of Marque; The Thirteen-Gun Salute; The Nutmeg of Consolation; Clarissa Oakes; The Wine-Dark Sea; The Commodore; The Yellow Admiral; The Hundred Days; Blue at the Mizzen; The Final Unfinished Voyage of Jack Aubrey*   48

C. P. Snow, The 'Strangers and Brothers' series; *The Two Cultures*   70

Rex Stout, *Fer-de-Lance*   86

E. B. White, *Stuart Little*   76

Coming attractions . . .

JUSTIN MAROZZI takes the road to Mandalay

MELISSA HARRISON explores Gilbert White's Selborne

DAVID RAIN is touched by Platero the Donkey

ANNABEL WALKER wings it

MICHAEL HOLROYD meets *The Smith of Smiths*

SOPHIE BREESE discovers a secret bookroom in Marrakesh

PATRICK WELLAND enters a Roman Emperor's world

BEL MOONEY ventures into *The Forbidden Zone*

The Royal Society *of* Literature

Tuesday, 9 December: Lionel Shriver in conversation with Fiametta Rocco
The Orange Prize-winning novelist, and author of *We need to talk about Kevin*,
reflects on being an American novelist who has chosen not to live in America, on
the state of American fiction and her scepticism about creative writing degrees,
and on why she likes to craft characters who are hard to love.
7 p.m. Kenneth Clark Lecture Theatre, Courtauld Institute, Somerset House

Thursday, 19 February: Claire Harman on Robert Louis Stevenson
Award-winning biographer Claire Harman reflects on John Singer Sargent's 1885
portrait of Robert Louis Stevenson, whom Sargent described as 'the most intense
creature I have ever met'. She talks about the circumstances under which the
painting was made, the friendships it reflected and its capturing of a moment in
Stevenson's life just before his own notable composition of *Dr Jekyll and Mr Hyde*.
7 p.m. National Portrait Gallery

For booking information on the above events please visit www.rslit.org or call 020
7845 4678.